CD INCLUDED!

BLUES

GUITAR LESSON ANTHOLOGY

A GUIDE TO PLAYING GENUINE HOUSEROCKIN' MUSIC

BY RICH DELGROSSO

ISBN 978-1-4234-8165-2

HAL•LEONARD®
CORPORATION

7777 W. BLUEMOUND RD. P.O. BOX 13819 MILWAUKEE, WI 53213

In Australia Contact:
Hal Leonard Australia Pty. Ltd.
4 Lentara Court
Cheltenham, Victoria, 3192 Australia
Email: ausadmin@halleonard.com.au

Visit Hal Leonard Online at
www.halleonard.com

INTRODUCTION

This is not a guitar method book. It's not everything you need to know about blues guitar. It's a collection of lessons that have withstood the test of time and have been appreciated by students over three decades. The lessons are organized into four chapters. With a mix of beginner, intermediate, and advanced skill levels, everyone will find something they can use. First are the grooves—basic rhythms of the blues. The second chapter focuses on playing melody lines and lead guitar parts. Some of these arrangements are presented as duets so you can practice them with the CD or with a friend.

Both chapters 1 and 2 may be played with a flatpick, but if you really want to play down and dirty blues, you need to learn to play fingerstyle, which is covered in Chapter 3. If you watch the blues greats—the pre-war pioneers or modern day greats—you will find that many play fingerstyle (watch Muddy Waters, Howlin' Wolf, Hubert Sumlin, Son House, or Buddy Guy). Using your thumb and fingers opens all kinds of possibilities, especially if you want to play a solo arrangement that combines a hard-driving bass and melody at the same time. Fingerstyle is worth the time and effort; you won't be disappointed.

The final chapter is dedicated to bottleneck slide. Slide playing in the blues goes back to the roots. It was a player in 1910, in Tutwiler, Mississippi, who sat and played slide with a knife blade on the strings, and consequently inspired W.C. Handy to pick up the blues. It's believed that this style was preceded by people building and playing a "diddley bow"—a crude instrument consisting of a string attached to a plank of wood, raised by "bridges" at each end, strummed and scraped by a knife slide or rounded object. Eventually, people discovered that the neck removed from a bottle fit the finger neatly and was easier to control.

The slide chapter is divided into three parts. In the first, you'll work on slide playing in standard tuning, playing melodies with single notes and/or double stops, and focusing on proper slide technique. Playing in standard tuning allows you to play slide without retuning your guitar. If your goal is to play in a solo style, then open tunings are what you want. The two most popular tunings are open G and open D; each presents different possibilities and different "voices." Mastering all three (standard tuning, open G, and open D) makes you incredibly versatile.

TABLE OF CONTENTS

Chapter 1 | THE GROOVES

The Boogie Bass Track 2

Beginner

This is a basic blues groove and a staple of blues, rock, rockabilly, and country players. It also serves as a good exercise in training your fingers to hold the position needed to play the different rhythms and box patterns in other lessons. Position your hand so that your index finger plays notes at the second fret and your ring finger plays notes at the fourth fret.

We start with the low, open E. The progression then ascends, descends, and repeats. The same finger position applies to the A chord, however, the riff peaks with the open G♮, which is a blue note (the flatted 7th). On the B7 (measure 9), the pattern breaks from the original and starts with the 2nd scale degree, F♯. Notice the chromatic note (A♯) that's included in the ascent to the V root (B).

4

The shuffle is a dance rhythm of the blues in which dancers "shuffle" their feet and sway to the music. Every blues and rock guitarist plays a box shuffle at some point. I placed the shuffle in 12/8 to capture the correct syncopation, with the notes on the downbeats sustaining slightly longer than those on the upbeats. Play the notes on the fifth string with your index and ring fingers. Strum through the sixth and fifth strings to add the open E on bass. Mute the strings slightly with the palm of your picking hand to give the pulse a more percussive sound. The same techniques apply to the IV chord (A7) as you shift to the fifth and fourth strings.

The difficulty in the shuffle is maintaining the pattern on the V chord (B7). Hold the index and ring fingers in place while reaching out with your pinky to grab the G♯. (It works best if you change the angle of your fretting hand so that your thumb is planted in the center of the neck.) Some players prefer to fret the B and F♯ with their first and second fingers instead; try both ways to see which feels more comfortable. Note the walk-up on the fifth string at the end during the "turnaround" (measure 12). Ending on B7 signals that the music is returning to the top or "turning around."

As you play the shuffle, lay back on the beat and don't push it forward. My buddies call this shuffle the "grinder" because we lay it down thick and heavy. It needs a strong pulse.

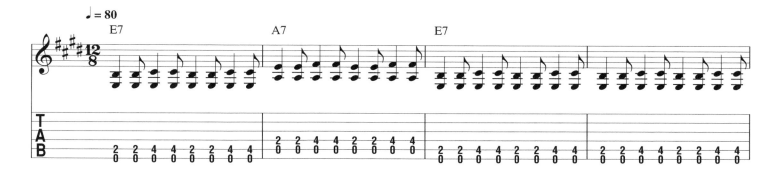

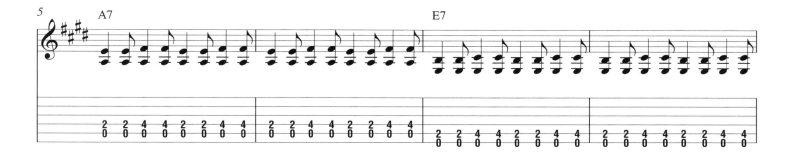

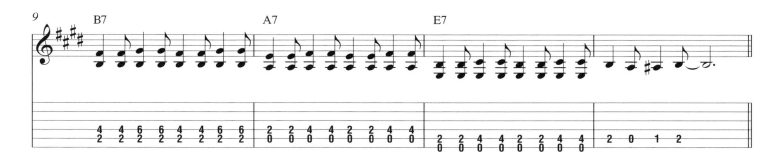

The great Jimmy Reed may not have been the first to break the shuffle up into this "loping" pattern, but everybody recognizes him for it. This shuffle is basically the same as the previous one, but the syncopation is different. The strings are separate, with the bass string plucked on the upbeat (the "&" when counting "1-& 2-& 3-&, etc."), and the note on the adjacent string is firmly on the downbeat. I've also added a variation in which the pattern of measures 4, 6, 8, and 10 adds ♭7ths to the progression. You can palm mute the strings in this progression (to make the rhythm more percussive) or leave them open.

This lesson has a turnaround at the end, but I've expanded it to include a riff that is a blues staple. In measure 11, you break from the rhythm to play what I call a "walk-down" riff in triplets. Fret with your middle finger on the third string and your ring finger on the first. With each beat, the triplet descends ("walks down") chromatically until you reach the tonic E chord. You then walk the bass up to the B7 turnaround.

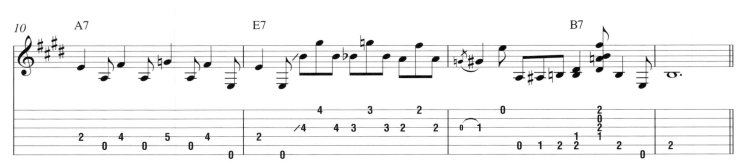

As Muddy Waters once said, "The blues had a baby and they named it rock and roll." This could be because Chuck Berry was a labelmate of Muddy's at Chess Records, and he helped popularize the "straight-eighth" shuffle. Here, the pulse is even without the syncopation of the shuffle. You'll find this style of "grinder" easiest to play in the key of A, as all three chord patterns (I, IV, and V) can be accessed with open strings on each bass. Easy!

I rated this one for the intermediate player because I gave the pulse a bit of a kick: I've added a tie at the end of each measure so that the last upbeat carries over to the first downbeat of the next measure. And on the V chord (E7 in measures 9 and 10), the rhythm breaks into a bass run. Once again, you may palm mute the strings in this progression or leave them open. Note the absence of the turnaround; not every blues contains one. It's nice to have diversity in your set if you're playing nothing but 12-bars—just make sure everyone in the band is on the same page.

This arrangement features a "walking" bass, as the bass line (bottom staff) outlines the harmony with a mix of arpeggios and scale runs. You can use the same finger positions that you used in the previous lessons, and a palm mute on the bass gives the rhythm more punch.

The guitar part on the top staff is "comping" chords (playing short chords or "voicings," in a rhythmic pattern). You'll find two variations for the seventh chord: The first is the conventional voicing—a triangle-shaped chord on three strings. The E7 is played at the seventh fret, with your middle finger on the fifth string, index finger on the fourth, and ring finger on the third. The other seventh chord is less common, as the three-note voicing doubles the 3rd with the ♭7th in the middle. The A7 in measure 2, for example, has a C♯ on the bottom, G♮ in the middle, and C♯ on top. This is a partial voicing.

The E+ chord in measure 4 is a transition chord that moves the progression from the I to the IV. It places your hand in a higher position for another A7 voicing. You then drop back down at the end of measure 6 to return to the E7 in measure 7. In measure 9, the partial A7 voicing is transposed up a whole step for B7 and slides back down to A7 before returning home.

Listening to the music of Chicago's south side players, like Jimmy Rogers, you find a wide range of rhythmic variations in the shuffle—all flowing from the same basic box pattern. One prominent feature distinguishes this shuffle from the others: the bass line rises from the root to the ♭3rd, and then to the natural third. This creates a powerful, forward-moving pulse.

On beats 3 and 9, a quick upbeat rake of the open first and second strings adds a punch. Picking this rake with an upstroke gives it a bright counterbalance to the heavy-handed bass. You may play it with a pick or fingerstyle.

This is a bit harder than it looks. It's best to fret the notes with an index-finger barre, covering the fifth and fourth strings (for the E chord) at the second fret. To ensure the clear sound of the upbeat "rake," angle your fretting hand so that it doesn't mute the second and first strings. The same technique works on the A6, but you can barre all of the strings at the second fret. The B7 is a standard open chord form that you hold in place and break up with a syncopation of the rhythm. Finish by returning to the A6 and the E, with no turnaround at the end.

Taking the blues back to its roots reveals a groove that's simple and raw in structure, but packed with the sensual musical energy. This groove is again bass-driven, with a rake on the upbeat. Each bar features a repeating riff with a rolling lick played on beat 4 by hammering on the B♭ from A, and pulling it off in a rolling motion through to the open G string and down to the E on the fourth string. Mastering this technique takes time, which is the reason for the advanced rating.

Note the slight bend on the G note in the opening riffs. In the key of E, G♯ is the 3rd and G♮ is the ♭3rd—a "blue" note. A blues guitarist, wanting to hear the dissonance created between these two notes, can bend the string to find that "note" in between. The blue notes (the ♭3rd, ♭7th, and ♭5th scale intervals) give the music the tension and dissonance we recognize in the blues. Give blue notes special attention—always! On the IV chord (A7 in measures 5 and 6), the same technique is applied, as the bass run rises to G natural (the flatted seventh) and ends measure 5 with a quarter-step bend on C♮—the bluesy ♭3rd in reference to A. For the B7 chord in measure 9, the riff stresses the bent D♮ (the ♭3rd of B).

Notice that, for the most part, the eighth notes are swung in this example (note the swung eighths notation at the beginning). However, at times the eighth notes are played straight to mix up the feel—just the way early blues pioneers did it. Listen to the audio to hear this mixing of swung and straight feel.

Extra: It's clear from the research and the writing dedicated to the blues that it was born in Mississippi—specifically the "Delta"—an agricultural region bounded by the Yazoo and Mississippi rivers. The earliest recordings from the late teens and early twenties demonstrate a variety of styles having developed in this region. This arrangement goes to the heart of Delta blues. If you hear a hint of Chicago blues, remember that in the great 1940s migration northward, African Americans from Mississippi rode the trains north to Chicago. Amplified, electrified Delta blues became Chicago blues.

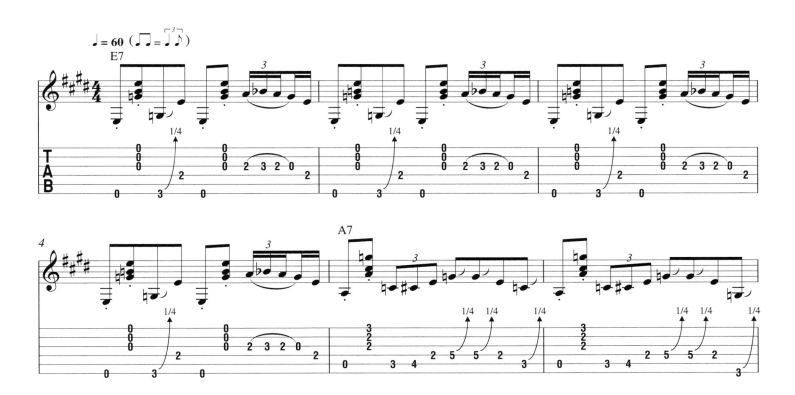

The Stroll

Track 9

Advanced duet

This groove is a complete departure from the shuffle. It swings as the bass riff glides from the root to the 3rd. There is no doubt that you'll recognize it from a host of rhythm and blues songs. My bass players call it a "stroll," but there may be other descriptions. Written in the key of C, it's a great change of pace all around.

I've kept it simple, focusing on the movement of the bass notes. The key is to play the second note of the pattern by sliding up to it on the same string. You open by picking the C on the fifth string and then slide up to the E at the seventh fret. You then finish the phrase on the fourth string in the same hand position (fifth position). The same pattern applies to the IV and V chords as they shift to the bottom strings. Once you master the syncopation, you have it all.

The lead guitar line is more complex. It comes in on the IV chord (F7), riffing off the F7 chord voicing on the third and second strings. Use your middle finger as the pivot on the third string, fifth fret, and your index finger on the E♭, second string, fourth fret. Maintain the finger position for the phrase in measure 6, with your ring finger sliding the F up to and back from the G♭ blue note. The phrase resolves in measure 7 on the E♮ (the C chord's major 3rd) and is then followed by a barred C6 voicing that slides down a whole step to become C9. As the melody progresses to the V (G7), use the box pattern for the C blues scale at the eighth fret, slightly bending the double stop to create dissonance. The melody finishes with a chromatic walk-down lick (G–G♭–F–E♭) that resolves to a somewhat jazzy-sounding major 3rd–root move (E–C). This ending lick is a typical one found in many blues and jazz tunes.

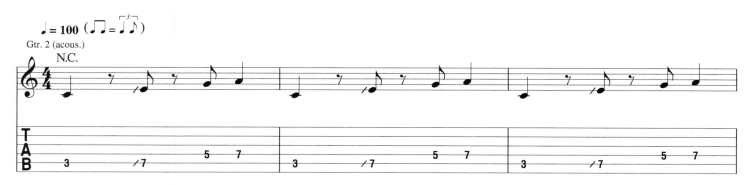

Another popular blues, rock, and R&B groove, this features the 7#9 chord, which is a type of altered dominant chord—a very tense sounding chord. Place your middle finger on the fifth string, fifth fret, your index on the fourth string, fourth fret, your ring finger on the third string, fifth fret, and your pinky on the second string, sixth fret. The chords are played syncopated and crisp, followed by the booming bass riff. Start this riff in third position, with your ring finger on the sixth string, fifth fret to play the A. However, fret the final D note of the measure with your middle finger to set you back up for the D7#9 chord.

The G7 (IV) is a form derived from the E-form barre chord. (We're just muting the fourth and first strings by not pressing down all the way with the barre (first finger)). The F (♭7th) on top of this voicing sustains the sound of the #9. The following riff is played with the index and ring finger, all in third position. When the A7 (V) comes around, I like to break from the groove with a run from the D blues scale (D–F–G–A♭–A–C) that carries over into the IV, and then drop back into the original D7#9.

14

When T-Bone Walker moved from Texas to the west coast, he ignited a new trend in the blues, giving rise to "west coast guitar," which was championed by Pee Wee Crayton, Gatemouth Brown, Hollywood Fats, and others. This style is characterized by a jazzier sound that is driven largely by ninth chords (as opposed to seventh chords in standard blues). This lesson is just a taste of what can be played on guitar. I use it in beginner/intermediate skill workshops, so it isn't very difficult to master.

Measures 1 and 2 demonstrate two forms (or voicings) of the ninth chord. The first form is a "rootless" G9 (does not contain G) and is an extremely common form in this genre. The fingering, from low to high, is as follows: index, ring finger, middle, pinky. The 9th of this G9 form is the A note on the third string, second fret. The C9 form in measure 2 is a complete ninth chord, with the root on the bottom. Start with the basic, triangular C7th chord (middle finger on fifth string, index finger on fourth string, and ring finger on third string), but also flatten (barre) your ring finger to cover the second and first strings as well. The 9th is the D note on the second string, third fret.

Measures 3 and 4 feature chord changes that were popularized by Walker, and are still utilized by many west coast players today. Likewise, the minor seventh chord progression through measures 7–9 is a popular transition technique. The use of ninth chords and minor sevenths are regarded as connections between blues and jazz guitar. I play the minor seventh forms with my middle finger on the bass (which also mutes string 5) and my ring finger barring the first four strings.

This groove comes from Chicago's west side, where players like Buddy Guy and Magic Sam popularized the minor key blues in the post-war era. As in the previous lesson, it's all about barres establishing hand position. For the Gm7, your hand is positioned at the third fret with an index-finger barre. This will set up perfectly to play the minor scale box pattern that follows. It's similar to the line you played in the first lesson (page 4), only it's in a minor key.

Maintaining the same hand position and index barre, you can easily shift the progression vertically to the Cm chord in measures 5 and 6. To play the riff in measure 6, slide your ring finger up to the D♭ and back down. The same hand/chord position applies to the Dm as you shift your hand to the fifth fret.

Building on the previous lesson, you can use barre chords to expand the minor sound and make it even more dynamic. To play this chord-based riff, first establish your hand position with an index-finger barre at the fifth fret. Your ring finger then barres the triads at the seventh and eighth frets. Once again, the work is done by the index and ring fingers.

For the pick-up, fret both the fourth string, fifth fret (G) with your index finger, and the A with your ring finger at the seventh fret. Pick the A and pull your ring finger off. In the same sweeping motion, "hammer" your ring finger back on the A, creating three distinct notes with one picking action. This is called a "pull-off" and a "hammer-on." The same pull-off works at the end of measure 2, creating a free-flowing melody line down to the D9 chord.

In this progression, D9 is a substitute for Dm, and your ring finger barres at the fifth fret. The same technique applies to the E9 at the seventh fret.

17

The Lower Voice
Track 14

Intermediate

Watching my students improvise solos, I find them consistently aiming high on the neck and ignoring the lower octave. This exercise works what I call the "lower voice." The opening riffs come from the C major blues scale, starting with the fifth (G). Note that I repeat the riff over the IV chord (F9). Playing the same phrase over the I and IV chord is a rule to keep in mind when improvising over the blues (and all the music born from it).

The melody line in measure 3 demonstrates how you can build on the box scale, working both vertically and horizontally. In the third position, you reach the tonic (C) and then progress back down the neck to the lower octave in the first position.

The phrasing over the C9 places strong emphasis on the blue notes—the B♭ (♭7th) and E♭ (♭3rd)—this provides tension in the melody. The melody in measure 8 ends with a phrase you will play often in the blues—the 3rd (E) followed by the root (C) above. The walk-down to the turnaround, starting with triplets in measure 11, is similar to the walk-down in the Track 4 lesson (page 6); this time it is played on the fourth and second strings.

Here we pick up on the previous lesson and expand it. Rhythm is critical to the blues. Hearing and feeling the beat is most important. The melody in this solo begins on the backbeat. The C9 at the end of the first full measure is also played on the backbeat and ahead of the chord change, which lends excitement, as it's unexpected.

I use this lesson to demonstrate building a melody that moves horizontally and vertically across the fretboard. You start in the first position, primarily on the middle strings. When the progression shifts to C9 in measure 5, you start with the box scale at the seventh fret. The return to the root (G7) brings you back down to the nut. In measures 8 and 9, the melody reverses and takes you to the D box scale that starts on the fourth string, fifth fret. It reverses again with the double stops (measure 10) and ends with a well-worn R&B phrase, and an even more common turnaround: ♭VI (E♭9)—V (D9).

As you work horizontally up the neck, your melodies create greater tension. The melody in this lesson is played over the same groove as the previous example, but it is more syncopated. It also builds in intensity as you move about the fingerboard.

Your hand begins in position at the third fret for both the G9 and the C9. The phrase in measure 4 comes from the music of west coast pioneers T-Bone Walker and Pee Wee Crayton. To get the most out of the phrase, barre with your index finger at the third fret and bend the C with your ring finger. Bending notes makes for smooth transitions and flowing, expressive riffs.

The melody rises in measure 7 as you focus on the first two strings. Position your hand to play the D9 double stop by barring with your index finger at the fifth fret. The subsequent phrase ends with your ring finger on D (third string, seventh fret). In transition to C9, play the D# at the end of measure 9 with your middle finger and slide it up to the E. Now, you are in the middle of the C major blues scale at the eighth fret. You can hang there as the chord returns to G9, and finish with what my buddies and I call a "big blues finish"—stepping the 9th chord down chromatically from A to G.

Shufflin' Double Stops

Track 17

Melody lines need not always be single notes. You can create an entirely different sound and groove with double stops. Double-stop melodies add variety and interest. A "double stop" is a two-note voicing—an incomplete chord that has the "voice" of the chord. This lesson features a double-stop solo played on the second and third strings.

You begin by rocking back and forth between the A and E9 in a shuffle rhythm, with your hand position at fret 5. The top notes are the E and F#, octaves of the notes you shuffled over the A in the "Shuffle in E" lesson from page 5, only this time the C# is played on the bottom. Measures 5 and 6 recall the pattern from the "Loping Shuffle" lesson on page 6, where you shift to the ♭7th midstream. It breaks the monotony of the rhythm riff.

Sometimes it's good to break from the rhythm altogether. This melody line, without the chord voicings, starts with a pick-up to the G# at the ninth fret (measure 9). The melody then drops down to E at the fifth fret, setting you up to play a phrase out of the D box scale. You are also in position to take over on the A and restore the original rhythmic riff. Coming back to it provides continuity.

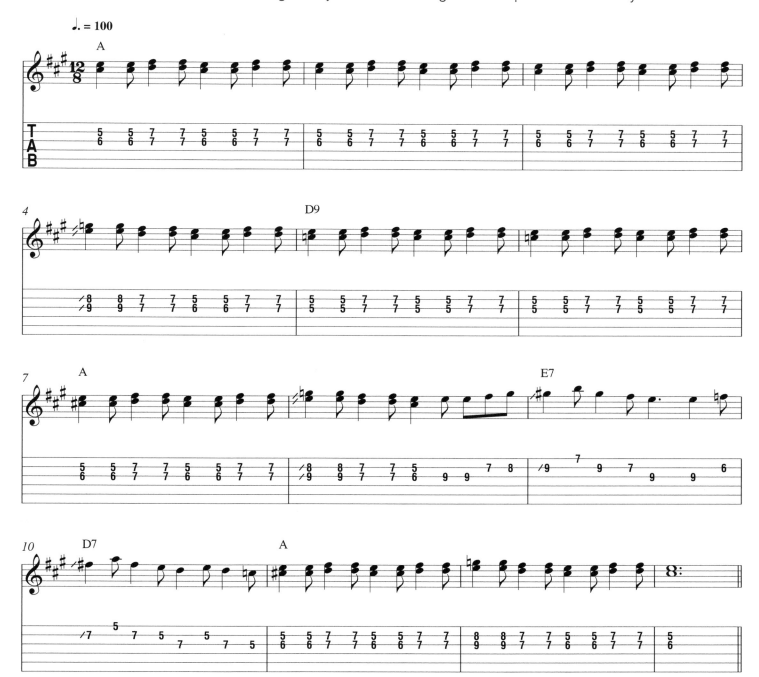

This duet reinforces the work you have done with the shuffle rhythm and develops a melodic concept (based primarily on basic chord structures). Gtr. 2 plays a straight-ahead shuffle in A. For the I, IV, and V chords, your index and ring fingers rock back and forth with open stings on the bottom. The only time you break from the rhythm is at the end, when you "turn" it around on the V (E7).

Gtr. 1 builds a solo that relies heavily on chord structure. You can use chords to build phrases at many different levels. To start, the D7 chord form played in the first position (at the nut) transposes easily to A7 at the ninth fret. This is the opening chord in measure 1.

The D major chord may also be played at the seventh fret. I call this chord the "A form," because its structure is the simple A chord in the first position—middle finger on the third string, ring finger on the second string, and the open E string. Now move this chord up the neck so that your index finger is on the first string, fifth fret, your middle finger is on the third string, seventh fret, and your ring finger is on the second string, seventh fret. You have now transposed the simple A chord to D. The phrase in measure 2 comes from this chord. The same chord form is the basis for the phrase in measure 4, this time using the octave of the original A (index finger on the first string, twelfth fret). The pull-offs and bends make the melody more fluid and add tension to the blues.

The melody drops quickly down the neck as your hand returns to the fifth fret position in measure 5, and then to first position in measure 7. To increase tension, give the E7 in measure 9 a more strident tone by doubling the open E with the E on the second string, fifth fret. A blue note is again stressed in measure 10, as you bend the C♯ slightly and repeatedly to create great blues dissonance.

This duet presents a soaring melody over a syncopated groove, a mix of comping chords, and a shuffling bassline. The groove features two chord voicings that are mirror images of each other. The G9 voicing forms a triangle shape on the fretboard with B, F♮, and A (low to high) at the corners. If you flip the triangle horizontally, you have another triangle with C, E, and B♭ (low to high) at the corners, which creates a C7 voicing. The same technique applies for the D9 in measure 9. To make the final measure more dynamic, I've broken from the rhythm to play chromatic triplets into a turnaround.

The opening phrase of this melody recalls a previous lesson where the D-chord form in the first position is transposed to G at the seventh fret. The melody is born out of this chord, working horizontally in a blues scale box pattern. The double stops in measure 4 walk the melody up to the barred C7 chord position at the eighth fret. It continues to rise to the root at the octave, this time using the "A form" chord (third string, twelfth fret). You then drop the same chord form down to the seventh fret for the melody in D.

Measure 10 is tricky, as you start out with the C7 chord at the eighth fret, jump to the fifth fret, resolve on G at the third fret, and then return and finish in the position you started at (the seventh fret)—lots of changes! The bends and slides make them more fluid.

Double Stops #2

Track 20

This lesson explores double-stop harmonies in 3rds. Note how the basic pattern in measures 1, 3, and 7 is altered to fit the IV chord in measures 2 and 5–6. The D♭/F dyad over the IV chord sounds particularly bluesy. For variety, I break out of the comping with a melody line over the V chord (D9) in measure 9, followed by strong hits on the B♭ in measure 10, and a final line that mixes the G major pentatonic and G blues scales.

Melodic development is all about hand and finger position. At first glance, this melody is daunting, with huge jumps that are frets apart. But if you begin with a barred D6 chord at the seventh fret, with your thumb planted squarely in the back center of the neck, the notes in the melody fall effortlessly into place. Slide the F♯ pickup into position. Holding the barre with your index finger, play the melody with your barred index finger, middle, and pinky. Each phrase ends with a release of the barre to grab the F♯ to restart the cycle.

As the progression shifts to the IV (G7), the melody line comes out of the barred G major chord at the third fret. In measure 7, the melody shifts to the D chord in first position at the nut. I use the same technique on the V (A7) in measure 9. In walking up the third string, use your index finger to play the B and your middle finger to play the C♮. Slide the middle finger up to C♯ to facilitate the position for the A7 barre. On beat 4, walking the first string down chromatically to the G7 position by using your index finger for the A, A♭, and G notes. On beat 3 in measure 10, it's best to play the B open to facilitate the playing of the F–F♯ move. The twelve bars end with a reprise of the melody played in measure 7.

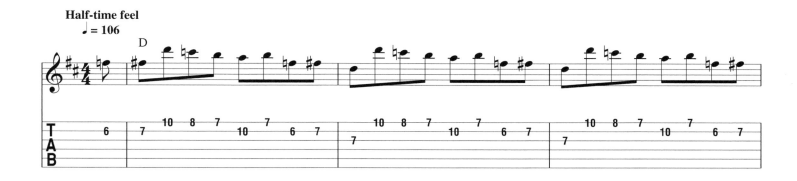

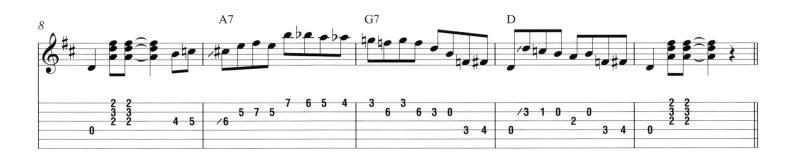

Circle of Fifths

This is the first eight-bar arrangement in the collection and the first to feature a "Circle of Fifths." The eight-bar blues is the foundation of many great songs like "How Long Blues," "My Baby's So Sweet," "Lonesome Day Blues," and more. The "eight bar" can be as simple as I–IV–V, or it can be jazzed up with minor chords or a circle of fifths. I wrote this for two guitars to introduce both the progression and one approach to building a melody over the changes.

The pulse of Gtr. 2 swings gently with a mix of bass notes and chords. It's easy to play, but you need a barred major chord. It takes practice and time to develop the finger strength to comfortably barre all of the strings at one fret. This arrangement opens with the barred G major and G7 chords. The IV chord, C6, is likewise barred to maintain the same hand position at the third fret. This time, barre the first four strings with your ring finger at the fifth fret. Shift your fingers to Cm while in the same position. Returning to the root, G, the progression flows ahead with the circle of fifths—a progression popular in the music of the twenties, as was the IV–iv change in measures 3–4. In the key of G, the "circle" typically begins by lowering the root three and a half steps from G to E. Then E is the 5th of A, which is the 5th of D, which is the 5th of G, so we're cycling through the dominant of each to get back to the I chord. This is sometimes called "backpedaling." To play the ninth chords, handle the lowest two notes with your second and first fingers, respectively, and then barre the third, second, and first strings with your ring finger.

As in previous lessons, the melody here is born out of chord forms—from the G major and G7 at the third fret, to the C major and C minor at the eighth fret. The melody in measure 5 returns to the G chord position and works, with some dissonance, over E9. The phrase over the A steps down to resolve on C, which is part of the D9 chord, and then progresses back to the G.

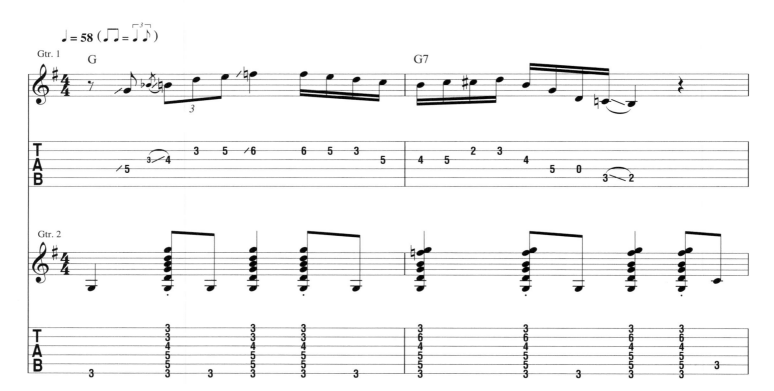

The golden age of Chicago blues was the era of Muddy Waters, Howlin' Wolf, Jimmy Rogers, Little Walter, and Willie Dixon. Their bands often featured more than one guitar player, and the magic of the music was the way the players worked together, playing lines that complemented and supported each other. Students often ask me for something different to play in a multi-guitar jam, and this arrangement gives you two approaches.

Gtr. 2 is a welcome break from the "same-old" shuffle pattern. It is a "boogie" bass line, like the first lesson in this compilation, but it has some twists and turns to give it more life. Note the "stutter" in measure 4, the rocking back and forth in measures 7 and 8, and how the stream of notes breaks up in measure 11, changing gears into the turnaround.

The lead line opens with a phrase built around a very dissonant Bb/D double stop. With each measure, the rhythm changes. Note the syncopation; the emphasis is on the backbeat. To capture this syncopation, practice first by reading the music and counting the downbeats out loud.

The melody riffs on the IV chord are born out of the C chord (the "A form" at the fifth fret). The Bb blue notes ride the crest and really stand out for effect. The progression returns to G7 at the third fret in measure 7. The V (D7) is presented in syncopated double stops. In measures 10 and 11, the phrasing contains a trill played with a hammer-on and pull-off. I position my hand to use my ring finger to play the Bb and my index and ring fingers to play the trill.

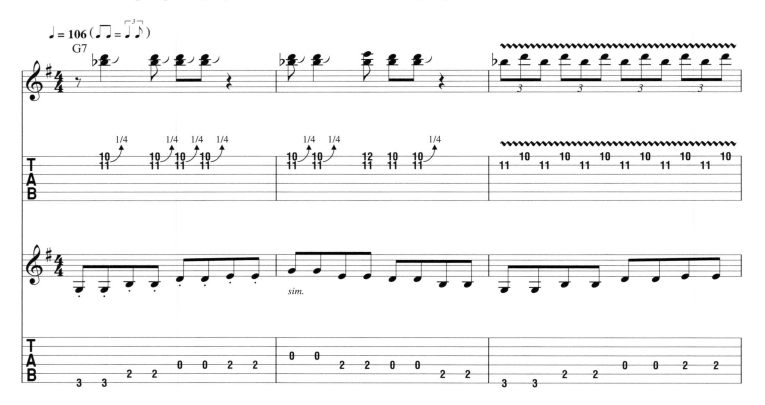

B.B. King is one of the most expressive guitarists in the blues kingdom, with a phrasing and tone copied by many. With this arrangement, I've tried to capture elements of his style, and unlike the other lessons where I've been navigating up and down the fretboard, this one plays a 12-bar melody all from one hand position!

The phrasing in this melody is unique in that it is centered, position-wise, on the IV chord at the eighth fret. The opening riff flows from what looks like the C major blues scale, ending with a G/E jab on the second and third strings. Remember that we're in the key of G though, so that's where the phrases will ultimately resolve. The rest of the melody follows suit, with your hand maintaining position and weaving between the overlapping scales. It's a unique, efficient way to play!

String bending is key to the style, as it adds both fluidity and tension. The half-step bends allow the melody to roll as it flows, while the whole-step bends make the notes really soar. Both types are accomplished with the ring finger pushing up. The whole-step bends require more energy, so you may find them difficult at first. The more you work them, the stronger you'll get, and in time you won't have to coax them as much.

Chapter 3

FINGERSTYLE BLUES

MONOTONIC BASS

Fingerstyle 101
Track 25

Beginner

Fingerstyle—i.e., the art of playing bass, chords, and melody at the same time—is the key to playing the blues, whether you play pre- or post-war, acoustic, or electric. The following are tried and true lessons that will get you started. The first series of lessons stresses the monotonic bass, which basically means sticking to only one string per chord in the bass.

The bass is the first part to master. Before you can play the melodies, you need to get the thumping of the bass to be automatic. Practice a strong, steady pulse by picking the open E with your thumb. By resting the pad at the base of your thumb against the string, you can mute the note so that it resonates less and is more percussive. Your thumb drives the beat, combining the bass guitar with the kick pedal on the drums.

Measure 2 begins the coordination between the thumb and index finger. Use your index finger to play the chords and melody by striking upwards on the strings. The very first beat is a pinch between your thumb and index finger, followed by two more strokes with your finger. Most players play these triplets with a quick slide into the first notes. The phrase ends by sliding down from B to A before picking the open G and the E on the fourth and third strings. This is a common riff, and you'll recognize it from the music of just about everybody—especially Lightnin' Hopkins.

Remember your first A chord played with three fingers on three strings? You won't use it in the blues. I've learned from the masters that an A7 chord, like the one in measure 6, is played with an index-finger barre. You will appreciate this chord in coming lessons, as the finger position gives you more range of movement and flexibility as you create riffs and phrases.

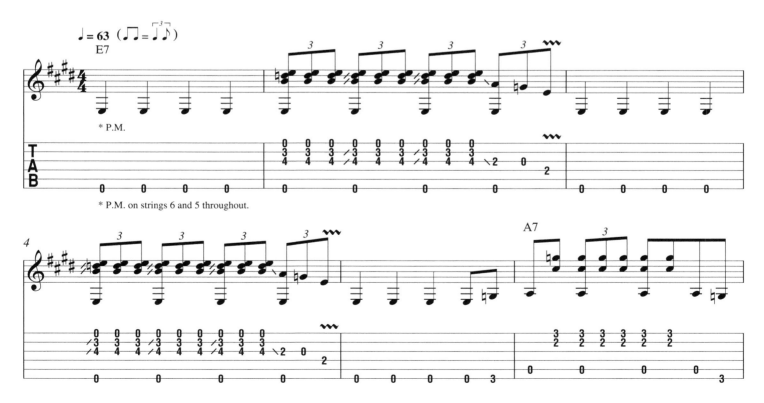

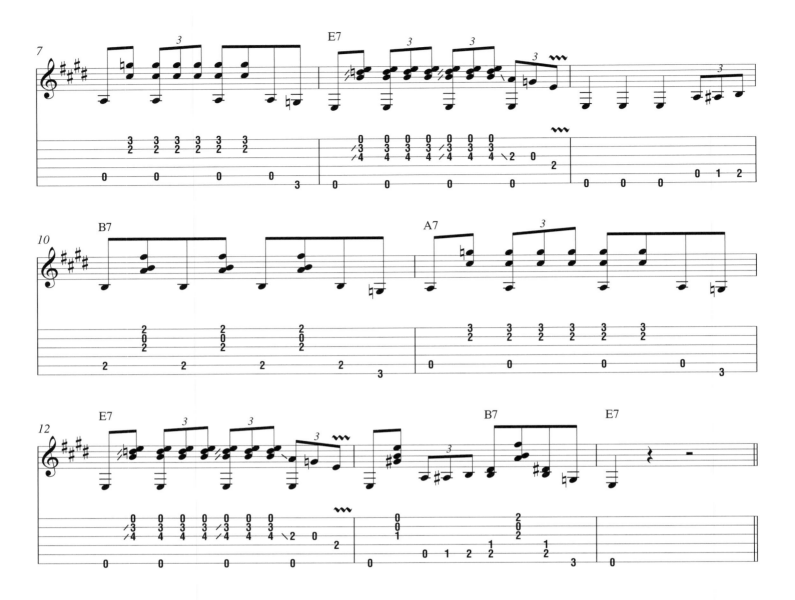

More than 12 Bars

Track 26

Intermediate

The 12-bar blues is the most common structure for the blues, but it's not the only one. This arrangement features the AAB poetry form, like a typical blues, but each line of the verse is separated by a repeating four-bar structure. And, unlike the other lessons, this one starts the melody on the IV chord. In a jam, from the bandstand, I would call out a IV–I–IV–I–V–IV–I progression.

A monotonic bass drives it forward, though it stutters on beat 2. When you get to the B7 in measure 11, you are playing the chord as a barre—similar to the A7, only two frets higher. It's very difficult to play a B in the bass with this voicing (you'd have to use your pinky on fret 7 of the low E string), so play the open-A string and mute it to a dull thump.

The repeating four-bar structure is built out of a riff that shifts between E and A, the barred A/C# double stop played with your middle finger. For beats 3 and 4, you return to E, hammer on the G#, step up to the ♭7th (D) on the second string, and then finish off with E on the first string.

The phrasing in measure 5 demonstrates the importance of an index-finger-barred A7 chord. While you hold the barred chord, the melody comes together as you fret with your index, middle finger, and pinky. Your picking hand thumps the bass rock-steady with your thumb. Train yourself to pick notes on the first string with your middle finger and the notes on the second string with your index finger. The same fretting and picking techniques apply to the V7 (B7) in measure 11.

This shuffle combines the best elements of previous lessons into what my friends and I call a "Texas Shuffle." You basically play a walking bass while raking the treble strings on the upbeats. I like to bookend the two-bar phrases with a triplet run at the end. Play the barred double stop on strings 2 and 3, followed by the open G and the E on the fourth and third strings. This shuffle is not as easy as it looks, so give it time to work. The pattern remains the same as you progress to the IV chord, shifting the bass line to the fifth, fourth, and third strings.

I decided to break away in measure 9, playing a bass run in triplets that starts with the pickup notes in measure 8. We glide through the V, the IV, and continue on back to the I and the turnaround. This turnaround flies by; it's very subtle and works whether the chords played by the band change or not.

This is a shuffle in the style of Otis "Lightnin' Slim" Hicks. It's a mix between the fingerstyle of Lightnin' Hopkins and the electric style of Jimmy Rogers. The bass still maintains a monotonic, driving force. The key here is the E7 double stop on the third and second strings. It powers the opening triplets and much of the melody as the lines weave in and out of the E chord.

As I play the bass on the A7, you'll hear it snap. My desire is a more percussive bass on this chord, so I angle my thumb under the string and snap it upwards. In transition from the E7 to A7 at the end of measure 4, I chose to walk the bass line up. There is a definite feeling of motion! The bass over the B7 follows a similar pattern. Starting with the B on the fifth string, it first shifts down to F♯ on the sixth string, and then walks up to the open A on the fifth string.

The phrase leading into the turnaround (measure 11) is the same as the Jimmy Reed turnaround ("Loping Shuffle," page 6), only fleshed out with double stops.

Blues in A

Track 29

Intermediate

In the key of A, the dominant bass is the open fifth string, once again played in a monotonic fashion. Recall the "More Than 12 Bars" lesson on page 34. This is a IV–I–IV–I–V–IV–I progression. It's in the style of one of the finest of all the fingerstyle blues performers: Big Bill Broonzy (see "Big Bill's Blues" lesson next).

The melody line in measures 1–2 and 5–6 is played over a D harmony, even though the bass is thumping out A. A is the 5th of D, and therefore, the bass line still works. The melody over the A chord in measures 3–4 is all in first position. You should approach the melody out of the barred A chord at the second fret. The index-finger barre makes the riff smooth and effortless. The melody over the E7 in measure 9 has a piano-blues feeling, and carries over into the D7 where the C♯ blue note is played with emphasis.

The walk-down to the ending is a classic "piano" line that sounds as if it's traveling in two directions at once—and it is! The bottom line on the fourth string walks down, while the top line on the second string walks up; the high A on the first string drones above. Maintain the high A note throughout with your pinky. Use your ring finger for the G note on beat 2, your ring/middle fingers for the F♯/D notes on beat 3, and your middle/ring fingers for the F♯/D♯ notes on beat 4. It's a bit tricky, so work at it slowly until it feels effortless.

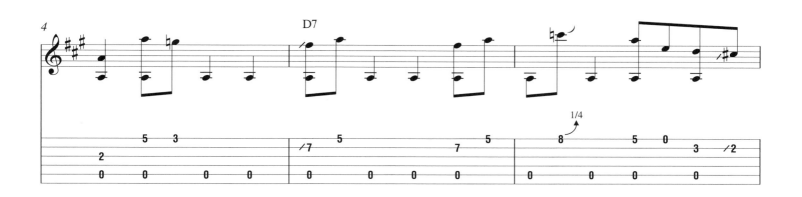

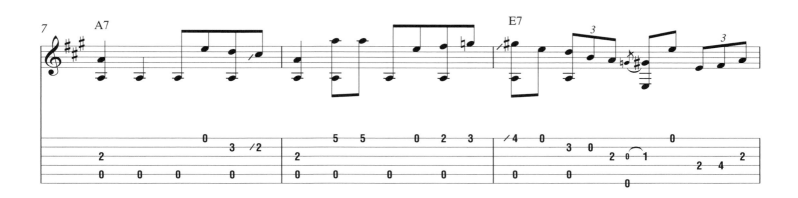

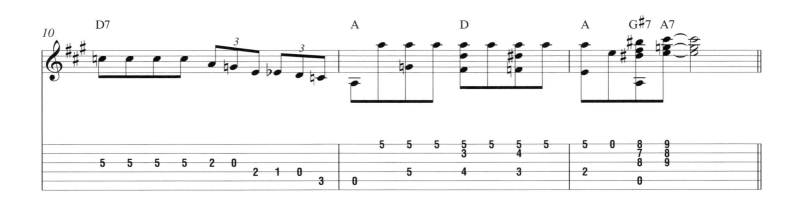

Big Bill's Blues

Track 30

Big Bill Broonzy was one of the most popular singers and songwriters in the blues, best known for his classics like "Key to the Highway" and "Willie Mae Blues." He was also was one of the finest fingerstylists of the era. This lesson, similar to the previous one, but more syncopated in its phrasing, continues to build on his style.

The opening riffs again come out of the D chord at the seventh fret, only they are played over the familiar A bass. The blues scales of the I and IV mesh together, and the unwritten rule in the music is: what you play on the I, you can usually play on the IV. Ending the phrase with a C♮, a blue note (the ♭3rd), adds a plaintive quality to the melody, especially as it hangs in space.

I'm certain you noticed that this arrangement has thirteen bars! Measure 4 is an extra measure. I use it as an example of how solo performers play from their heart and feeling, and not from their head and convention. They often drop or add beats and measures. They let the music flow out without counting.

The melody over the IV (D7) continues the theme of the opening lines, only increasing in complexity. The transition from the A7 to E7 (measure 9) features a bass line that flips over on itself—a technique that Broonzy used often. The ending returns to the original motif for symmetry.

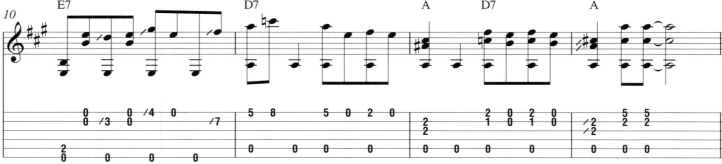

The Broonzy classic "Key to the Highway" is widely played and copied probably due more to its unique progression than anything else. When a singer sits in with a band and they have a song with this special eight-bar structure, they will most likely call out "Key to the Highway" or Brownie McGhee's "Crow Jane." But many other songs have been written with another eight-bar progression: I–V–IV–IV–I–V/IV–I–I. Unlike the standard 8-bar, this progression substitutes the V for the I in measure 2, hence the name "Quick to the Five."

The phrasing in measure 1 comes from the E chord and blues scale starting on the third string, ninth fret. This dissonant riff can be heard in countless recordings, both in pre- and post-war blues. Measure 2 drops the chord melody to the first position with the full B7 chord and is followed by two bars of A. It's best to barre the A chord with your index finger at the second fret, even as you walk the bass up the fifth string in measure 6 to play the C♯ on the bottom. Placing the C♯ (3rd) on the bottom of the A chord is a piano player favorite. When I hear a guitar player do it, I know they know the blues!

The arpeggiated seventh chords in measure 7 have the McGhee touch. It's structured as the common walk-down to the turnaround, but McGhee would lift his ring finger off the first string in the second chord. This changed the perceived direction of the notes, giving them an interesting twist!

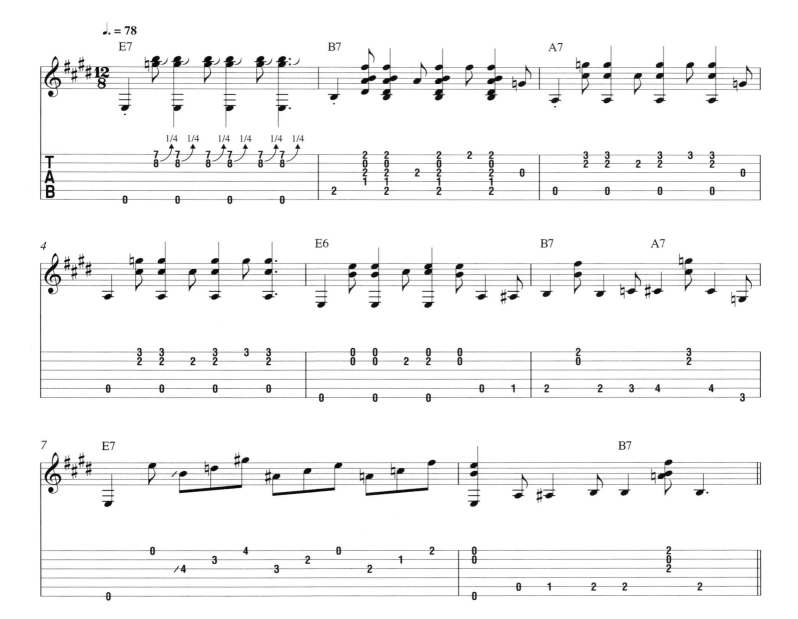

Another popular way to play the "Quick to the V" is to open with the E in first position, and then work horizontally up to the B chord barred with the index finger at the fourth fret. You play the high B and A with your pinky and middle finger, respectively. In this position, you can't fret the bass note B on the fifth string, so it works better to mute the open-A string to get a thumping pulse. Then, in measures 3 and 4, you use the same barred A chord at the second fret.

For variety, instead of the I–V–IV in measures 5 and 6, I've substituted a circle of fifths progression. Here, I use a mixture of picking and strumming. I pick up with my index finger on the backbeat of beat 1 and strike the strings on beat 2 with the top of my nails on my middle and ring fingers. The "old-timers" called this type of picking "frailing." I repeat this technique with each chord change. Measure 7 features another twist—a McGhee technique where he would break from the triplet rhythm midway, giving the turnaround a whole different feel.

This is a rich mix of many of the previous lessons, with the added pulse of the monotonic bass. My favorite feature is the double stops on the first two strings, which makes a good lesson in working the fretboard.

The opening double stops are part of a seventh chord voicing; it's actually the same notes you've played in the first position on the third and second strings, only up an octave. The voicings walk down in triplets by scale tones, including the ♭7th (D♮). They resolve at the seventh fret with the "A form" chord for E (see "12-Bar Blues in A" lesson on page 22). To add dissonance and tension, slightly bend the G♮ (string 2, fret 8) instead of playing the G♯ (string 2, fret 9). You really want a note between these two. For that reason, you give the string a slight bend, which is known as a quarter-step bend. On the second pass, starting in measure 3, the voicings walk by scale tones all the way down to second position, with F♯ on top. The melody line over the A7 in measure 5 is derived from the A major chord barred at the fifth fret.

The chord changes in measures 9 and 10 are new for this series, and are inspired by the music of Earl Hooker and Freddy King. These voicings can be used in different keys for different chords. Notice how the first three-note chord shape on the top three strings resembles an open-position Dm chord. Move it to the seventh position with a B bass note, and it becomes a B6. In this move, we walk the voicing down chromatically, two half steps at a time. The same move is transposed down a whole step and repeated for the IV chord in measure 10. To facilitate the movement of these voicings while still maintaining the pulse, mute the E string down to a thump.

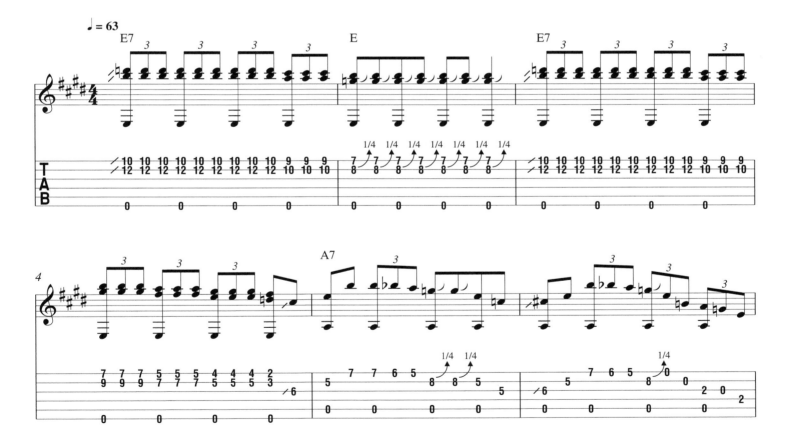

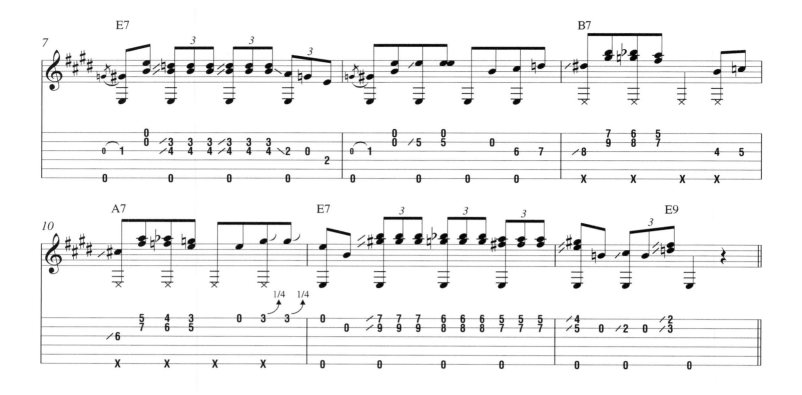

Double Stoppin' Texas Style

Track 34

Advanced

If you count the measures here, you'll find a very odd number: eleven! This may have started out as a conventional 12-bar blues, but I deleted one of the IV chord measures (A7). This is another example of how a solo performer can take the music in their direction of choice and not be confined by convention. Lightnin' Hopkins was one of the best of the "unconventional" performers. He would often take a standard double-stop melody line and break it up into different phrases.

Like the last arrangement, you open with the octave seventh chord double stop, only to drop down to the first position in measure 2. Then, you jump back up to the octave with a weaving phrase born out of the E minor pentatonic scale. Dropping the thumping bass really highlights the tension of the solo.

The A7 in measure 5 is a barred chord at the second fret, as explained in earlier lessons. Doubling the E note in measure 6 gives the melody more character. This piece has great dynamics, as you start high in the octaves and cascade down to the lowest tones. There is also similarity and symmetry in the phrasing.

In previous lessons, we've used double stops to add harmony to riffs and phrases, but they're also useful in creating harmony in song melodies. In this lesson, I've chosen an old folk melody that some call "Betty and Dupree" as an example.

Recall the double-stop patterns in the previous lesson. We will now use the same technique on the fourth and third strings. There are basically two structures to the double stop—one in which your fingers are separated by a fret (i.e., B and G♯), and another in which they are adjacent (i.e., C♯ and A). Use your index and ring fingers to fret the notes in the former, and your index and middle fingers for the latter. As you horizontally move on the string, your fingers will shift positions.

The melody over the A7 in measure 2 is an arpeggio best played using the index-barred chord at the second fret. This measure, combined with the first, makes up the first line of the verse. There is a space of two bars before the next line. Rather than leave it empty, I've added what is called a "fill." You'll recognize this phrase, as it's based on the turnaround you first worked on in "The Loping Shuffle," only this time, it's played in harmony as duplets with the open E on the first string. To play the phrases in measures 9 and 10, use the B and A major chords played as index-barred chords.

The double stops in this lesson are separated by a string and played with a pinch between the thumb and index fingers. Each of the phrases begins in the previous measure with a pick up note—a bass note played on the backbeat by the thumb. Your thumb then jumps to the adjacent string to begin the phrase. The melody is played on the fifth string, and you harmonize with 6ths played (coincidentally) on the third string. As in the previous lesson, you alternate your fretting middle and ring fingers as the chords move horizontally back and forth. Repeat this pattern in measures 3, 4, 7, 8, 11, and 12.

For this arrangement, it's better not to barre on the second fret for the A in measure 2. Use your middle and ring fingers, low to high. The notes on the fourth and second strings create harmony in 6ths on top. As you move ahead, alternate fretting on the second string with your index and ring fingers. This pattern is repeated in measures 5, 6, and 10. The technique is the same for the B chord, only starting at the fourth fret. Again, it's very difficult to play a B in the bass, so I've substituted with the open A string. It's dissonant, but then again, it is the blues.

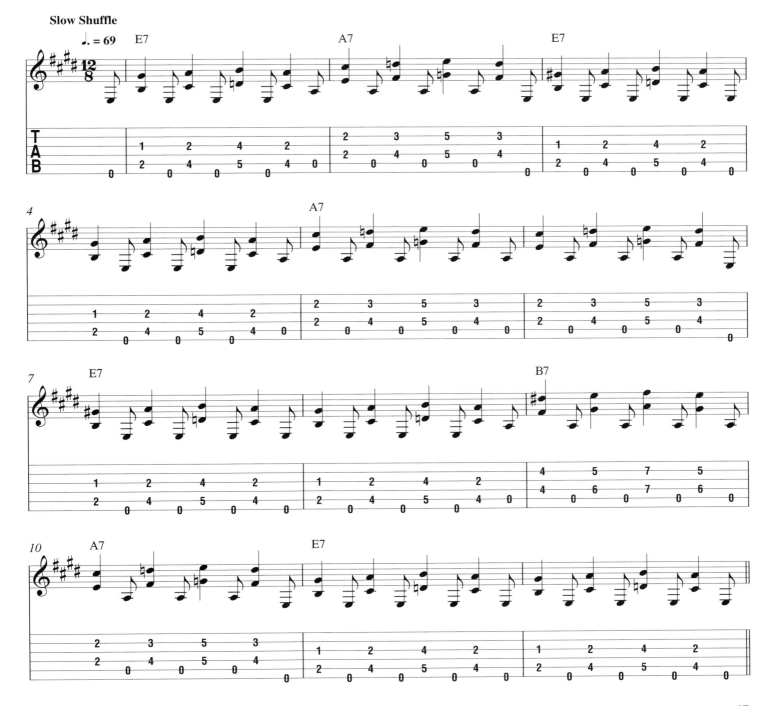

John Lee Hooker was the master of the boogie, and I use this lesson to introduce fundamentals of his style. A boogie rhythm can be played in standard tuning, but Hooker and others preferred an open tuning to get the full sound of open strings—especially on the bass and mid-range. There are many different open tunings. This tuning is called "Spanish" because it was the tuning of a very popular twenties-era guitar piece called "Spanish Fandango." It's an open G tuning; tune the E strings down to D, and tune the A string down to G.

To get the groove, you strum down on the fifth and fourth strings with your thumb, and strum up on the third string with your index finger. Practice the groove until it's steady. Hooker was the consummate solo performer; his singing and picking followed his heart—he didn't count beats. Some phrases added beats to measures, while others dropped beats. As an example, I've dropped a beat in some measures where I leave the groove to play a riff. These phrases break the rhythm into 9/8 and are played with steady, monotonic bass notes.

I've included several different phrases—rich with blues notes. In this tuning, you find them at the third fret. The ♭3rd (B♭) is found on the third and fifth strings, and the ♭7th (F♮) is found on the first, fourth, and sixth strings. Play the notes at the first fret with your index finger and the notes at the third with your ring finger. In measure 7, start with your index finger on the C, but then slide it up to the D, flatten it over the first string to play the F♮, and then slide it back to the C. The seventh-chord double stop in measure 9 works best as an index-finger barre, so you can slide down to the C on the last beat.

Hooker often stressed the "lower voice" of the guitar. Here, a riff on the bass opens with pickup notes in measure 12. Watch the tempo; you drop a beat in the second measure of the riff. Last, but not least, the riffs in measures 15 and 16 are my favorite. Start with an index barre at the third fret and slide your finger down to the C; fret the B♭ with your ring finger.

Open G tuning:
(low to high) D–G–D–G–B–D

Slow Shuffle
♩. = 65

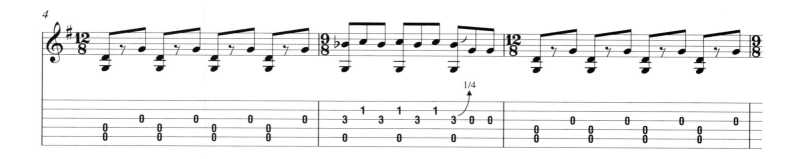

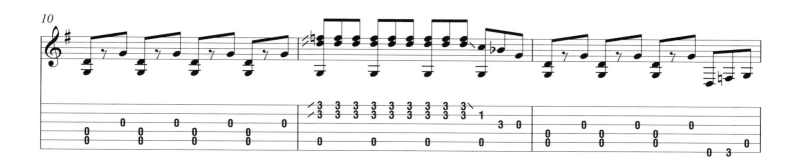

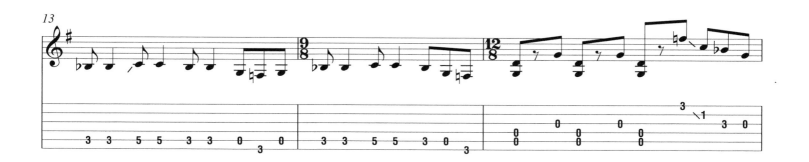

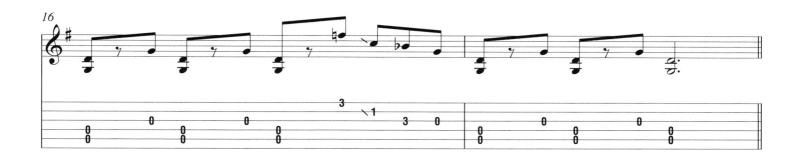

Droppin' the D

This arrangement recalls earlier lessons, but has a deeper, darker color to it. The opening riff should be familiar, but you'll find it placed a whole step down from previous lessons. This is possible in standard tuning when you lower the sixth string down to D. This is called "Drop D tuning."

The opening riff is the same one we have used in other lessons: a seventh-chord voicing played in triplets. The phrase in measure 2 comes from the D blues scale that begins on the third string, seventh fret—the "A form" chord for D. The ideas are then repeated in phrases in measures 3 and 4.

In measure 5, the melody in G emerges from the G major chord at the third fret. Note the bass: when the sixth string is tuned down to D, G is now at the fifth fret, and it is very difficult to play the melody while fretting the bass. I play the G on the first beat of each measure to give a "taste" of the chord and then follow up with the muted string to maintain the pulse.

Using an index barre at the second fret for the A7 chord (measure 9) facilitates the chromatic walk-down the first string—pinky to ring to middle finger. The rolling grace notes in measure 10 are hammered on and pulled off. The extravagant ending, with the chromatically descending sixth chords, is played with a ring-finger barre of the first four strings.

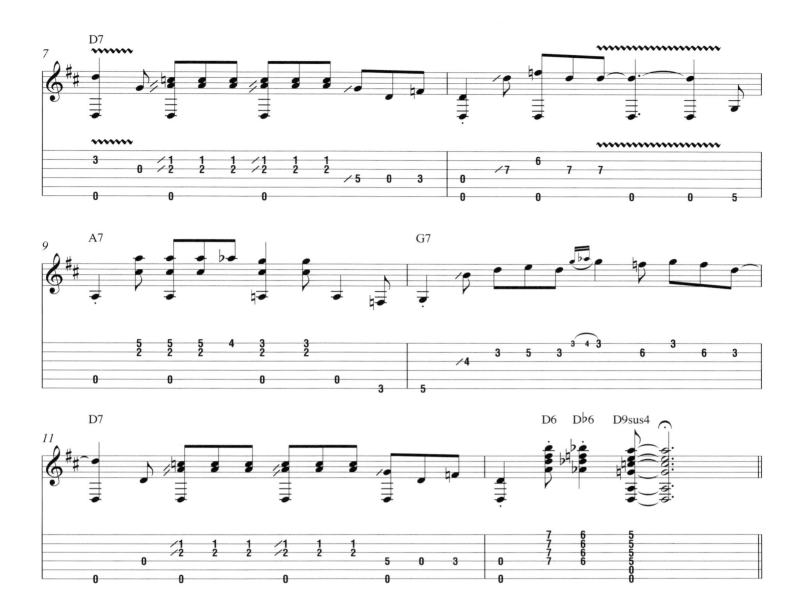

Taking the tuning a little further—try what is called "cross tuning." In this instance, it's a mix of open G tuning and standard: (low to high) D–G–D–G–B–E. Playing in the key of D with this tuning gives you open bass notes on the I and the IV.

For this one, I've adopted some techniques from the music of Lonnie Johnson, one of the finest twenties-era musicians and regarded as the creator of the single-string solo in blues and jazz guitar. I should add that the tuning is my idea (not Johnson's), but it works really well with his melodic structure.

The double-stop triplets recall previous lessons. This time I chose to raise and lower them over the first four measures. In measures 5 and 6, adding the A on top of the G results in a Gadd9 chord—an interesting tension not commonly heard in the blues. Note the use of the open G on the bass.

The riff in measure 7 is sophisticated and tricky. I play the D with my index finger, and after bending the E to F♮, my index finger drops down to barre the second fret and then drops again to play the G♯. Work the timing slowly until you master it. Measure 8 presents a very different voicing for the D7, with the ♭7th (C♮) on the bottom and the fifth (A) on top! For the V (A) chord passage in measure 9, once again, it's best to barre the strings at the second fret, this time including the fifth string for the bass. Using diminished chords in the turnaround (measure 11) was a Johnson trademark and a common feature of music in the thirties.

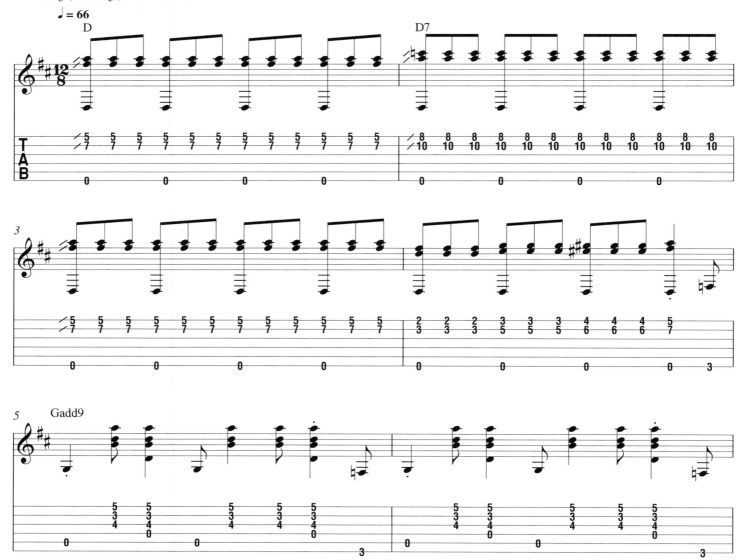

52

I've explored the techniques of Bill Broonzy in previous lessons. He was one of the finest fingerstyle blues guitarists of the forties and fifties, so I can't resist another lesson! Broonzy was a master of the monotonic bass, and if you've been following the sequence in this compilation, you should be getting comfortable with your thumb pounding the rhythm on a single string. You may have found the technique slowing you down as you explore melodies, but I believe this lesson will give you some newfound direction.

Consider the opening bars, all in C, in the first position. The melody line comes from the major blues scale, ending with the smear, E♭ to E. You could play this line while holding down the C on the fifth string, but with this hand position, grabbing the E♭ is a stretch. The melody flows freely if you play the open fifth string on the bass, muting it to get a "thump." It works melodically, as A is a scale tone, and I believe it actually makes things more interesting.

On the Fadd9 in measures 5–6, you may barre the full chord, but I prefer to leave the bass as a fully muted open string. It allows me the freedom to leave the chord position and vamp on a different line while still maintaining the pulse. I also love Broonzy's different chord voicings, as heard in measure 7 where the C is played with a G on top. It's especially hip how that G note carries over from the Fadd9 in previous measures.

In measure 11, you find Broonzy's approach to walking down through the turnaround. Unlike other turnarounds in the series, this one employs major chord double stops, (as opposed to seventh chords) walking down chromatically. Take note that not every song that features a turnaround actually ends on the V. This arrangement continues on with the tonic.

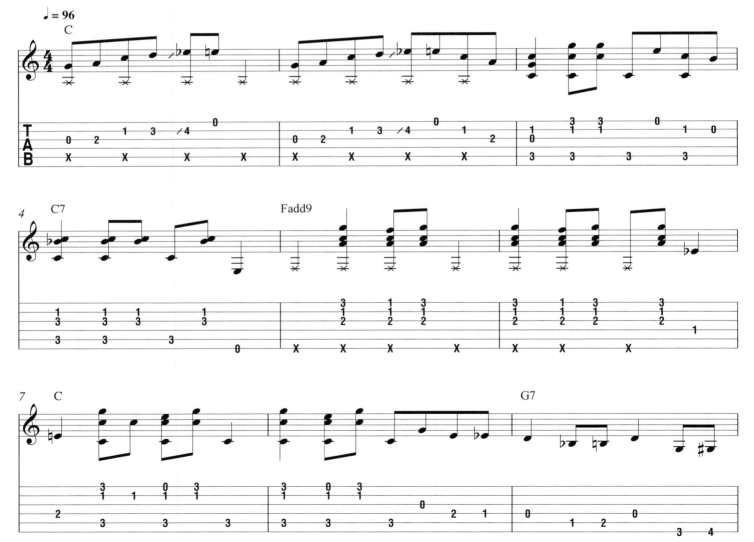

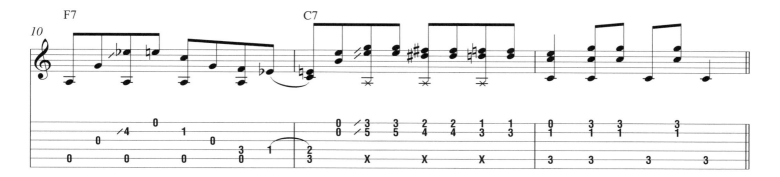

Key of A

Track 41

Intermediate

The key of A is a natural for the monotonic bass, though it does take time and practice to grab the fifth string instead of the sixth. As you did when you started fingerstyle, practice thumping the bass until you can play it without thinking. Now, while your thumb keeps the beat, play the A7 chord at the ninth fret. This is a chord I introduced with the "12-Bar Blues in A" lesson on page 22. Let it ring out above the pulse. The progression is "quick-to-the-four," so you move to the IV chord in measure 2 and then back to the tonic in measure 3. Here is a technique that Muddy Waters favored: he often lowered the seventh chord one fret, or one half step, to simulate a quick-to-the-four change. The resulting chord, played over the band's D7 backing harmony, is actually a very dissonant D#°7 that works great!

Returning to the A7, play triplets, and then while changing gears to arpeggiated 6ths, walk the riff down. And speaking of dissonance, the use of C♮ on beats 3 and 4 (as opposed to the expected C#) may make you grimace, but that's the point! As you progress to D7 in measure 5, the melody works from the "A form" D chord at the 7th fret. To give the C in measure 5 an ever-so-slight bend, I stretch my hand to play it with my ring finger.

Don't forget the rule for playing A in the first position with an index-finger barre—it will make all the difference as you play measures 7 and 8. Release the barre as you play the E and G triplets, but bring it back for a strong finish. The melody over the IV and V chords (measures 9 and 10) is accomplished with the same "A form" chord technique as measure 5.

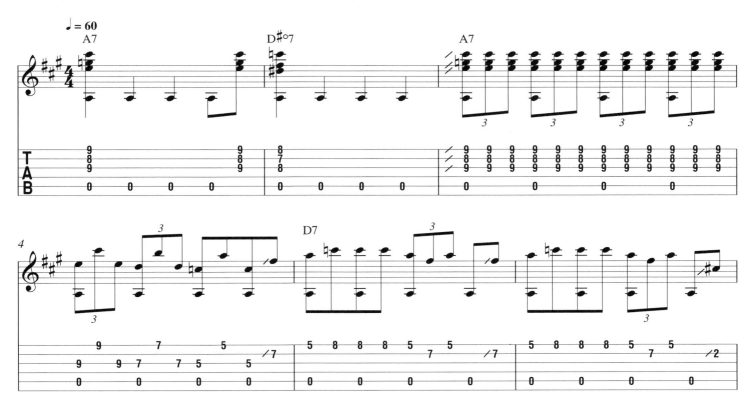

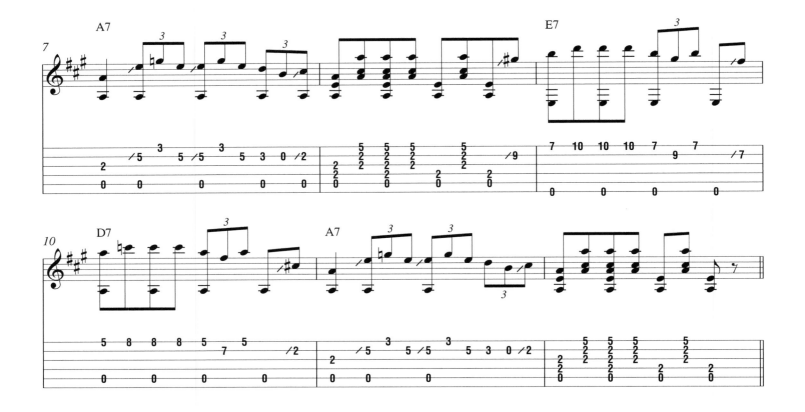

Carolina Blues
Track 42

Intermediate

Brownie McGhee was one of the finest fingerstyle players from the Piedmont—a geographic region that stretches from New Jersey down through the Carolinas and into Georgia. McGhee was heavily influenced by Blind Boy Fuller, and this arrangement captures some of this style.

The previous lesson gave you the basics. The opening four bars are similar enough, with changes in the timing and phrasing. But as the progression returns to the D7, the phrasing is somewhat acrobatic, as you have to jump to play the pickup bass notes in measure 4 and then leap to the seventh fret. The deep sound of the F♯ (3rd) on the bottom of the D7 chord sets the tone and is worth the effort.

McGhee often favored long, drawn-out bass runs like the one that dominates measures 7 through 10. As I pointed out in the electric section, it can be really refreshing to hear the melody played in the bass, and here you make the line soar down in the bottom! The walk-down in the turnaround is in the "piano style" that we've used in previous lessons, with the notes on the fourth string stepping down in pitch as the notes on the second string step up. It is best to play it from a barred A chord at the second fret.

ALTERNATING BASS

8-Bar Blues
Track 43

Beginner

Having mastered the monotonic bass, you're now ready for the alternating bass, where your thumb moves from string to string. Musicologists consider its origin to be the Piedmont, as its first practitioners came from the eastern seaboard of the U.S. I will refer to the style as Piedmont or alternating thumb. For this introduction, you'll play an 8-bar blues, likewise born in the Piedmont.

Next to the 12-bar, the 8-bar is the second most popular progression in the blues. We first explored it in the lesson titled "Circle of Fifths" (page 28). In this lesson, you'll use it to acquaint your thumb with the picking style. Try picking the sixth string and then the fourth string with your thumb. Repeat it over and over, keeping the pulse even. You need to train your thumb's muscle memory as it recalls the reach between these two strings.

As a simple intro to your new skill, strike the G on the bass with your thumb. On the second beat, frail the chord. "Frailing" is a chord strum technique where you brush down on the strings with the top of the nails of your middle and ring fingers. In fingerstyle, you have two other chord playing options: strumming down through the chord with your thumb, or strumming up with your index finger. Both options are awkward! Frailing allows your hand to move naturally. Then, on the backbeat, pick the G with your thumb as a pickup to the next beat. Your thumb then jumps to the open fourth string on the next beat, and your middle finger picks the G (fretted with your pinky) on the first string. Frail the chord on beat 4.

Apply the same pattern of picking and strumming to the chords in measures 1–6, changing the major chords to seventh chords. To prepare for the turnaround in measure 7, fret the G on the bass with your ring finger, and the G on top with your pinky. Then, with your thumb, walk the line down on the fourth string, fretting with your ring, middle, and index fingers. When you play the D7, use your fret-hand thumb to curl over the neck and play the F♯ in the bass. That's the blues.

Now that you have a sense of thumb movement in this style, it's time to take it up a notch. I searched my song memory for a progression that would provide long stretches of practice on different chords, and this one has worked for many of my students. This is a departure from the 12- and 8-bar blues. It's unique, but familiar, recognized from songs similar to "Last Fair Deal," a popular blues from the twenties and thirties. It's in the key of A, so your thumb will begin by alternating between the open fifth string and the fretted E on the fourth string. To play the chords, you "pinch" the strings, plucking the fourth string with your thumb, the second string with your index finger, and the first string with your middle finger.

For the E chord, the same picking and pinching rules apply, but your thumb shifts to the open sixth string and the E on the fourth string. The same applies to the D7 chord, only you curl your fret-hand thumb over the neck to play the F♯ on the sixth string. Your picking thumb alternates between the F♯ and the open D string. Practice this arrangement until you can play it without reading it. You want the thumb action to be automatic.

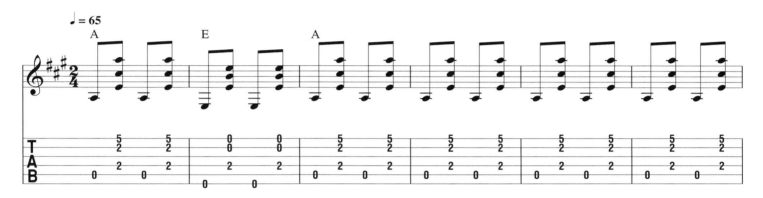

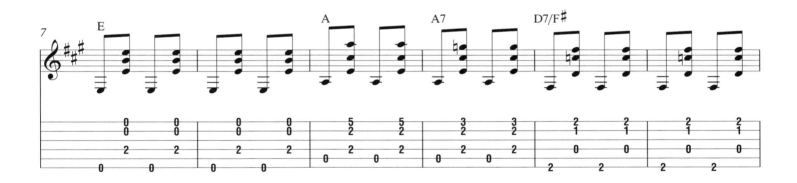

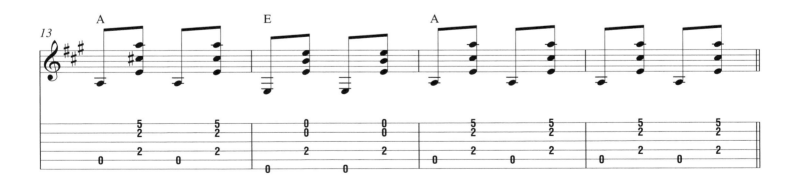

Piedmont Blues #2

Track 45

The Piedmont blues is often regarded as "ragtime" guitar. Ragtime rhythms are more complex and syncopated than the monotonic bass or alternating thumb techniques that you have practiced so far. Now you are ready to build on your skill. Use the pinch (thumb, index, and middle finger) to play the chords, but syncopate the second beat. On the downbeat, pluck with your thumb, then pinch the double stop on the first and second strings while plucking the fourth string with your thumb. The rhythm for the measure is as follows: count 1-& 2-e-&. As before, play the A chord as a barre at the second fret and curl your thumb for the bass on the D7 chord.

Now we're changing the time signature back to 4/4 time and the progression to IV–I–V–I. This is the progression of a host of country blues songs, such as Mississippi John Hurt's "Coffee Blues." We're also increasing the syncopation, though not at first. The first time through is basic Piedmont rhythm with syncopation only on the last beat of the measure: count 1-& 2-& 3-& 4-e-&. Remember to pick the notes on the first string with your middle finger. The D/F♯ chord has F♯s on both the top and bottom.

The second time through, starting in measure 6, is more syncopated on beats 2 and 4: count 1-&-a 2-e-& 3-&-a 4-e-&. To fill out the chords, as your thumb strikes the fourth string, strum harder to include the third string.

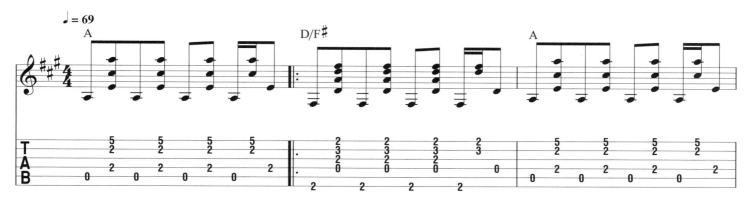

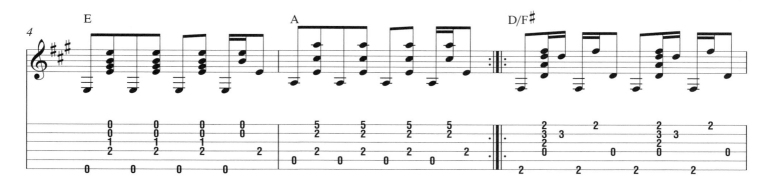

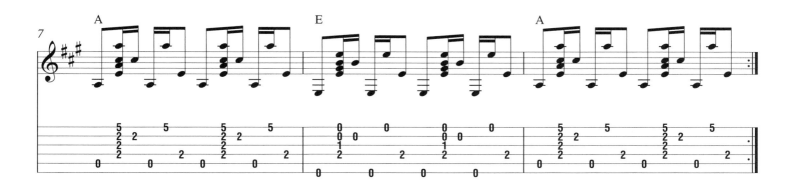

When playing fingerstyle in the key of D, the music is made richer by dropping the pitch of the sixth string from E to D. In this tuning, you have both the sixth and fourth strings tuned to D, allowing your thumb to alternate as before on the tonic (D) chord.

I've adopted the syncopation (reverting back to 2/4 time) of the "Piedmont Blues #2" lesson on page 60. The same picking rules apply: thumb on the bass strings, index finger on the second string, and middle on the first string. Note that for the G chord, the G on the bottom is at the fifth fret, due to the drop D tuning. This can be tricky, so, in measure 4, I like to lift my fingers off the D chord on the last beat to free my hands in readiness to change hand position for the G. I also like the sound of the open E on top of the G chord; it gives the chord a lighter feeling. To play the A chord, you revert back to your beginning guitar lessons and play with individual fingers (not the barre—the first time in this collection!). The picking rhythm is consistent throughout.

This is a sequel to the previous lesson. Here, you pull melody from other forms of the chords, starting with the "A form" for D at the seventh fret. Start by playing the alternating bass a few times to get into the rhythm. Slide into the F♯ with your ring finger and fret the A with your index. The same picking rules apply as before. For the rhythm of the first two measures, count 1-& 2-e-&-a, 1-& 2-&.

By measure 5, your fretting hand is changing back to first position. Fret the B with your ring finger, A with your index, and drop down to fret the F♯ with your index and D with your middle. Do the same in measure 6, but as you drop down, play the F♯ with your middle finger and C with your index.

For the G chord, your hand shifts to third position, with your ring finger on the bass (G) and your index finger fretting the melody. The progression returns to D in the first position. The measure in A is played with the traditional, non-barred A chord. The final phrase rolls off your index finger with the pull-off.

Track 49

The key to this arrangement is the first position E chord. Holding the E on the fourth string anchors your hand for smooth changes in the picking. To play the pickup phrase, pinch the open E and B. Count the rhythm: 1-& 2-e-&-a 3-& 4-&. Use your pinky to fret the C♯ as it darts in and out of the rolling rhythm.

The phrasing on the A chord is best played with an index-finger barre at the second fret to reach the high A with your pinky. Play the G♮ with your middle finger. The melody over the B7 comes directly from the first position B7 chord.

Circle the Fifths

Track 50

The circle of fifths has appeared in several previous lessons as a substitute for the V–IV bars near the end of an 8-bar and/or 12-bar arrangement. In this lesson, it's complete as a 4-bar arrangement in E. Yes, there are songs with this progression, like the bluegrass standard, "Let Me Be Your Salty Dog."

This arrangement is in the key of E and starts with the "circle." C♯ is the 5th of F♯, which is the fifth of B, which is the fifth of E. The opening pickups kick off the progression and are best played walking up the fifth string with the index, middle, and ring finger. The C♯7 chord is the same as C7 in the first position, only one fret higher, with your ring finger on the low C♯. The picking rhythm is 1-& 2-e-& 3-& 4-e-&. The F♯ chord is played as an index-finger barre chord at the second fret. B7 and E are standard first-position chords.

The second time through (beginning in measure 5), the bass alternates strings, playing the root and the 5th below on the C♯7 and B7 chords, and the root and 5th above on the F♯7 and E. The rhythm, the third time through (starting in measure 9), steps up the syncopation by adding bass lines in transition, walking up to the C♯7 and B7, and walking down to the F♯7 and E.

I love the raw, sensual energy of the music of the Mississippi hill country—its modal sound, with ringing open strings mixing with dissonant strategic blue notes. After listening to the guitar playing of Howlin' Wolf, I pieced together a series of themes that appear in his music. I've defined them here as patterns A through D. The basic rhythm pattern is 1-& 2-& 3-e-&-a 4-&. All four are played out of the open-E chord.

Note that the fourth string most often rings open as D♮, the ♭7th in the key of E. This allows you to leave the fingering of the chord form and emphasize other notes. Pattern A emphasizes the G♮ (♭3rd) on top. Pattern B drops the G down to D, placing emphasis on the ♭7th. In pattern C, the D is lowered to C♯, the 6th, and when added to a seventh chord, really rings dissonantly! Pattern D milks this dissonance by bringing in the C♯ on beats 2 and 3.

I recorded this arrangement on electric guitar to make the case for fingerstyle in the post-war blues. All of today's great players today use fingerstyle or a mix of fingers and picks.

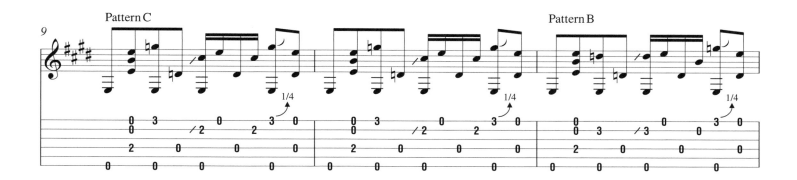

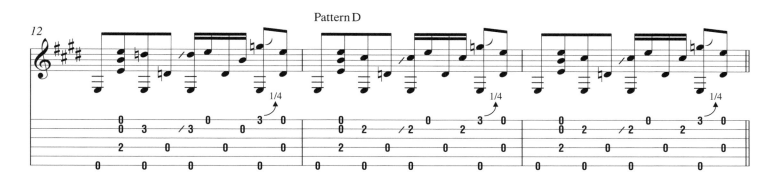

Chapter 4 | BOTTLENECK SLIDE

STANDARD TUNING

Slide in Standard #1
Track 52

Beginner

Nowadays, you may find real bottlenecks made of different kinds of glass, or tubes made of metal—some are even made from ceramic. I've even seen players with socket wrenches and medicine bottles! The style and weight of the tube is a personal choice. Glass does produce a different tone than metal. Louisiana Red, one of the slide greats and a protégé of Muddy Waters, literally has hundreds of slides. He tries everything he finds!

How to wear the slide is another personal choice. A few players wear it on the index finger, but this method is most limiting with regard to fretting notes normally, and it's not easy to control. Others, like Bonnie Raitt, wear the slide on the middle finger. This affords better control, as you're able to brace it with adjacent fingers, however, you're primarily limited to playing slide notes. Wearing a slide on the ring finger or pinky frees your other fingers to mix fretted notes and chords with slide notes. The pinky slide gives you the most freedom and is preferred by most players.

There's no need to re-tune the guitar to play with a bottleneck slide. In fact, playing in standard tuning is a good skill to have when you sit down to jam with other guitar players. The slide gives you a unique, different voice! The disadvantage, when compared to an open tuning, is that you need to stay mostly with single-string melodies and some double stops. You can add a monotonic bass if you play in E, A, or (sometimes) D. You don't have the freedom that an open tuning provides.

There are ample notes in the legend on page 102 regarding the symbols in the notation, but I'd like to point out some key references. When reading tab, the slanted lines indicate the direction of the slide. In most cases, you slide up or down into a note from just one or two frets below or above. The ⌇⌇ marking above a note calls for vibrato—a technique you will use for sustaining a note and giving it character. Moving the slide slightly and repeatedly back and forth along the string creates the vibrato effect and sustains the note.

Playing slide in standard can be tricky. You need to be careful to pick the notes you want played and not to pick other strings covered by the slide. Dragging your fret-hand index finger behind the slide helps to dampen the strings and stop them from sounding.

The opening melody comes from the E blues pentatonic scale at the octave. After sustaining the E with vibrato, walk it down the scale with alternating slides (up and down), resolving the phrase by sliding into the "A form" chord for E at the ninth fret. The following phrase stresses the B at the twelfth fret, only to step down chromatically to the E chord (and then the E7).

Measures 5–8 demonstrate a good "blues rule" to keep in mind when you are jamming: what you play on the I, you can usually play on the IV. The E blues pentatonic shares common tones with the A blues pentatonic. I've repeated the opening lines over the IV chord to demonstrate this. The walk-down during the turnaround is one you've played before. This piece doesn't turnaround, but features a unique ending—one that Muddy Waters played almost every time he played slide in standard tuning. A barred slide on the first three strings creates a sixth chord, and Waters would end the song by stepping the chord up from D6 to E6.

This arrangement expands on the previous lesson; you should recognize some phrases from other lessons as well. I often approach slide in standard by playing riffs I already know. They sound different though, because the slide is more expressive! For example, in measure 2, I like the smooth, turning motion of the G♮ gliding down to F♯ on the second string, and then sliding up to the E on the third string. The phrasing over A7 is another good example, as you play the melody out of the fifth-position A barre chord. You should recognize this phrase from previous fingerstyle lessons.

I use the slide to play the E in measure 7 and the B in measure 9 to sustain the notes with vibrato. You could pick the notes on open strings, but sliding into and sustaining them with vibrato has more intensity and feeling! This is a technique that you will use often in arrangements to come. Another well-worn phrase in the blues is the one at the end of measures 7 and 10. Pull off the A to the G♯, middle to index finger (without using the slide), pick the E on the fourth string, and then pluck the E octaves. I hear this in the music of many players, from Skip James to Lightnin' Hopkins.

Muddy Waters is one of my favorite slide players, both in open G and in standard. Here, I've put together some of his phrasing in standard. The melody line takes off at the octave, but is anchored by the E on the third string, ninth fret, which is part of the barred E6. Once again, I'm playing the E and B notes with the slide to sustain them with vibrato.

Note the trill in measures 6 and 7. Play the open-D string, then repeatedly hammer and pull off your middle finger on the same string at the second fret. Recall the phrase in the previous lesson, where I turned the notes from A to G♯ to E. This blues calls for a more modal sound, so you flatten the G♯ to G♮.

Waters also preferred to flip the walk-down turnaround in measure 11, making it "walk up"—a signature riff for Waters. You maintain the fingering of the E chord, pinching the fifth and third strings as you walk it up one fret per beat in triplets, with the open E at the center of each triplet.

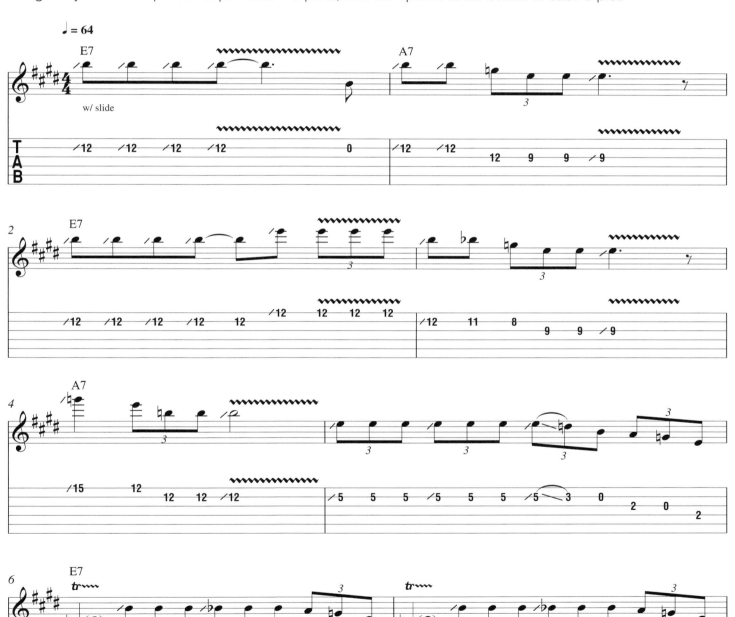

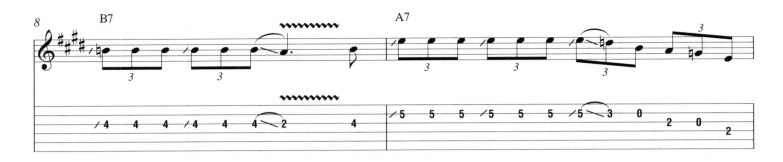

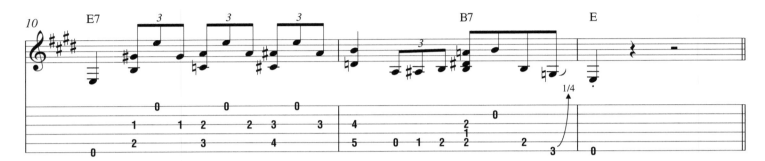

Nighthawk Track 55

Advanced

Robert Lee McCollum was a Mississippi native who became a guitar legend in Chicago as "Robert Nighthawk." His intricate, expressive slide lines are some of the best in standard tuning. This piece is a tribute to him and other great slide players like Tampa Red, Elmore James, and Will Weldon.

You open with slashing slide double stops at the twelfth fret, which is very reminiscent of James' hit songs like "Dust My Broom." The phrasing then takes a turn as you jump between the octaves, using the open E string to free your slide as you move down the neck. Note the mix of the open E and the fretted E in the phrasing of measures 3 and 4. The open E to slide E, with vibrato for sustain, is a phrase you hear a lot in the music of Nighthawk and Tampa Red. You really work that technique in this lesson.

Note how you play the G♯ in some phrases instead of the blue G♮ note, reserving the blue note for the times you want to be most dissonant. The same technique is applied on beats 2 of measures 4 and 8, sliding from E down one half step to D♯ instead of the ♭7th (D♮). That's the blues! I also like how the rhythm in this lesson often changes gears from triplets to duplets. Variety is the spice!

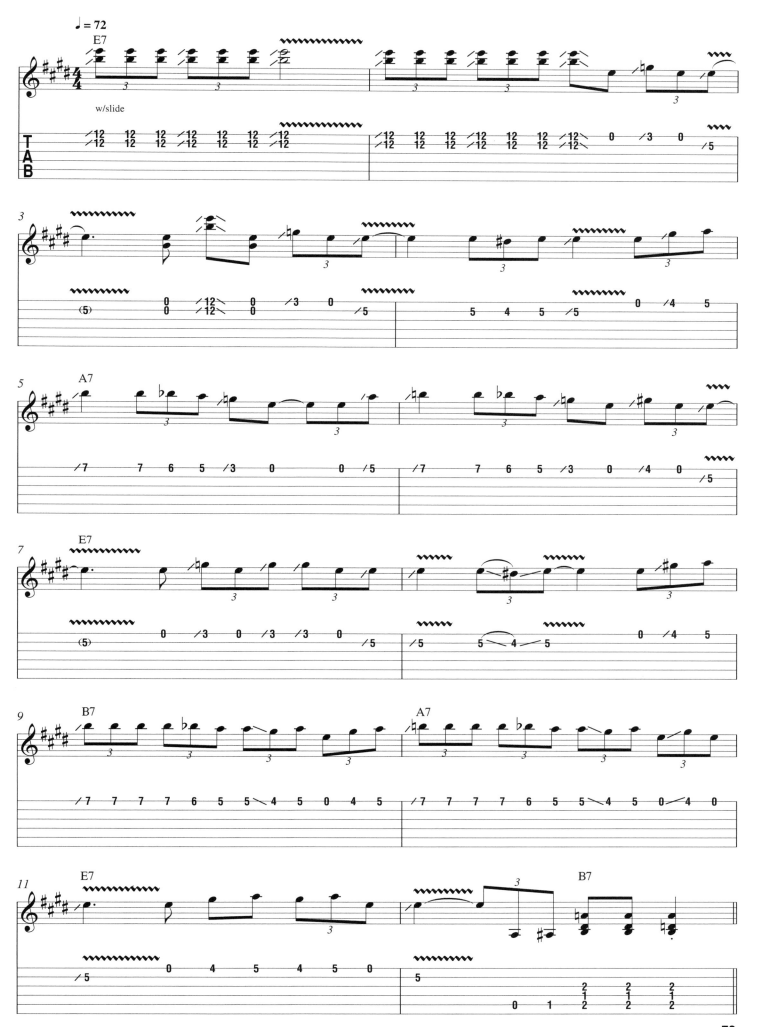

A simple technique like tuning the bass down to D can create a whole different sound for the guitar. In this lesson, Gtr. 2, which is in drop D tuning, establishes a dark, syncopated groove popular among New Orleans players known as "second-line" rhythm. At the core, is a partial D7th chord you hold in place momentarily before jumping to the F# (3rd) on the sixth string. The last phrase of the measure pulls your fingers back into position to repeat the chord. The playing on the G7 is parallel, but your index finger on the fourth string and ring finger on the sixth string form the chord. For the A7 (measure 9), barre the A chord at the second fret. The rest of the phrasing then flows easily out from the barre.

The phrasing of the lead guitar, Gtr. 1, is sparse, allowing the rhythm guitar line to come out. The focus of the melody is at the twelfth fret on the fourth string, with heavy emphasis on the blues notes F# and C#. You rock the line back and forth between the tenth and twelfth frets. Each "chorus" then ends with slashing slide on the F# on the fourth string, third fret.

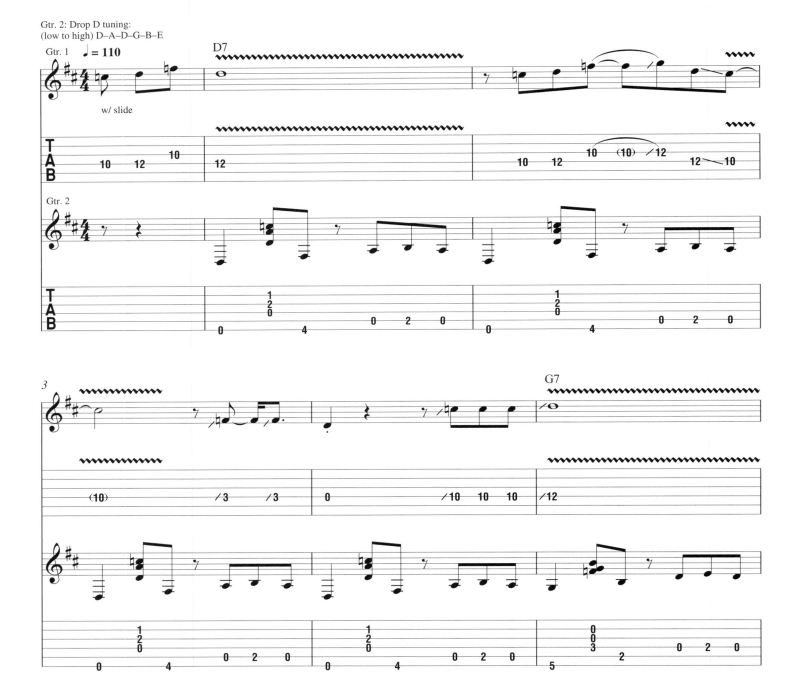

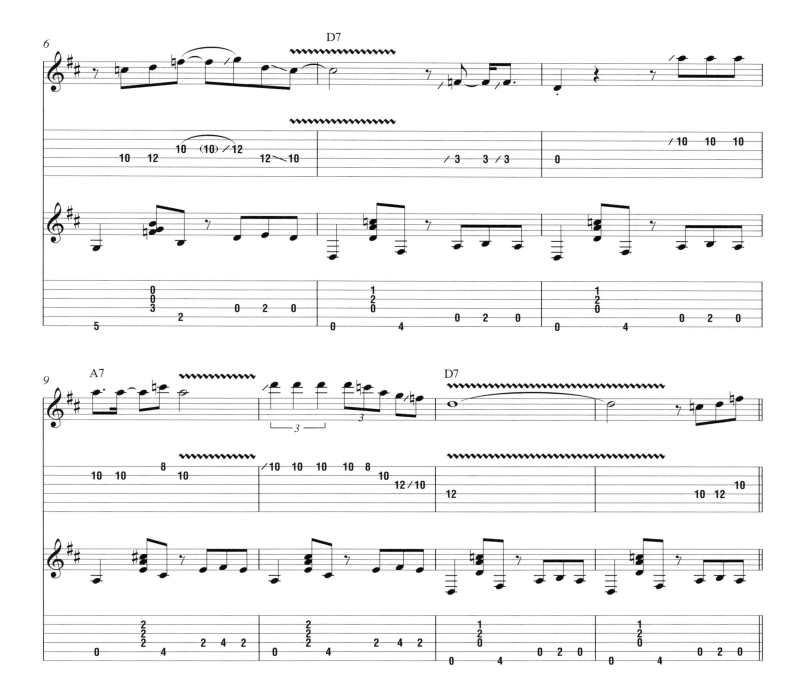

OPEN G TUNING

Slide in Open G Beginner

Track 57

The power of bottleneck slide really comes out in an open tuning. Tuned to an open chord, the guitar provides real options for bass lines and chords in a slide arrangement. One of the oldest tunings, often referred to as "Spanish" because of its use in a popular twenties' song called "Spanish Fandango," today it's better known as open G tuning. Low to high, the strings are tuned D–G–D–G–B–D. From standard, you tune the sixth and first strings down one step to D and the fifth string down one step to G.

To get you started, the focus of this lesson is a melody without bass and chords; subsequent lessons will be more complex. This arrangement is a simple beginning, with a basic melody that highlights the blue notes in the key of G: F♮ (♭7th) and B♭ (♭3rd). You will find these notes at the third fret.

The opening phrase begins with the sustained G with added vibrato. In measure 2, slide again into the G, slide down to the F♮, slide further down to the C on the second string, and then slide up to B♭ on the third string. For contrast, work the blues notes on the bass at the end of measure 3. Repeating the melody over the IV7 chord, you can add notes on the second string for sliding double stops.

In this open tuning, a barre across all of the strings at the fifth fret creates a C (IV) chord. The same technique applied at the seventh fret creates a D (V) chord. The phrasing in measure 9 comes from this chord position. We'll work this relationship more in lessons to come.

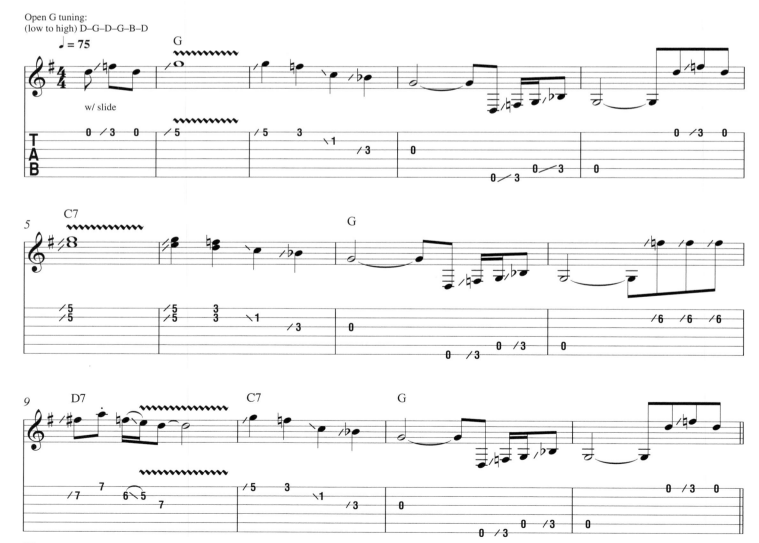

Much of pre-war blues came from the rural Mississippi and Piedmont areas, and is often referred to as a body of work called "Country Blues." The list of notable performers includes Eddie "Son" House, Charley Patton, Barbecue Bob, Blind Willie McTell, Fred McDowell, and Peetie Wheatstraw, to name a few. Their music can be considered the bible for modern-day performers, rich with grooves, riffs, and techniques.

The focus at first is the melody. Follow the slanted lines in the TAB for direction of the slide. In the previous lesson, I pointed out how you may play barred chords for the I, IV, and V with the slide in open G. You will also find chords in first position. The G (I) is easiest, as it is just open strings (see measure 7). The C (IV) is similar to the C chord in standard tuning, but without C on the fifth string (see measure 5). To keep it basic, play the fourth, third, and second strings. (Although, an open fifth string G works on the bottom too.) The open D notes (first and sixth strings) are too dissonant for a proper C chord and should normally be avoided. You'll find examples of the D and D7 (V and V7) chords in subsequent lessons.

This arrangement builds on the previous one. I've chosen a rudimentary melody that I hear in many songs from the period. It is an 8-bar blues with an introduction. The focus is still on building melody with chords filling in. I've also added some bass.

You may be surprised by the rhythm of the introduction. The second measure switches from 4/4 to 2/4 meter, resulting in two dropped beats. I want to bring attention to the fact that most recordings of solo performers from the pre-war era have arrangements with added or dropped beats. The solo performer is all about playing from the head and heart, and he/she may choose to move forward faster or hold a phrase a couple of beats longer. Be aware as you study the masters that you will occasionally encounter these timing puzzles. When you suspect a rhythm is changing gears, take time to count. You can find the measures where beats have been dropped or added.

In measure 3, I've added chords and bass to the melody. Note the technique on the bass. Leading into the chord, you pick the sixth string on the backbeat as a pickup to the chord. Playing the V–I on the bass followed by the chord was a popular technique in the country blues. I'm "frailing" the chords with the top of my nails. The D7 chord, in the first position, is the same as it is played in standard tuning: C♯ on the second string, A on the third, and open D on the fourth string. With this tuning, you add an open D on the first string. I didn't write the C chord with this technique, and I kept the bass on the fourth string, playing the 3rd (E) on the bottom like a piano player would invert the chord.

Elements of the melody should seem comfortable by now. Measure 9 features changes in the rhythm, a technique I hear a lot in the music of Tampa Red and Lonnie Johnson. Note the pull-off on the final beat of the measure.

Track 60

The attack in this tuning now shifts to the octave at the twelfth fret. The melody of the lesson is similar to Son House's "Special Rider Blues," and has a haunting quality to it, which is great for slide.

Work the phrase on beat 3 in measure 2. You're sliding up, down, and then back up, so make it flow smoothly. Be sure to dampen the strings behind the slide. A slight touch with the index finger cancels most of the overtones and allows the slide note to sound clearly. Try it with and without and note the difference in the sound.

This melody has two voices: the sweet slide at the octave and the rougher slide at the third fret towards the end of each "chorus" (as in measure 3). Practice giving these voices different energy and tension.

This is a lead guitar piece in open G tuning that you may play fingerstyle or with a flatpick. I recorded it with a second guitar to put in a duet context. As you recall in an earlier lesson, I explained how performers sometimes mess with progressions, dropping or adding beats and measures. In this example, I've taken an 8-bar blues and added a measure (the seventh measure). In a conventional 8-bar blues, the progression would turn from the V to the I, but here it's moving from the V to the IV to the I. This arrangement technique is not new. The most famous example I can think of is the classic "Sittin' on Top of the World," a hit recording for the Mississippi Sheiks; it's since been covered by many blues and bluegrass artists.

This piece stresses the blue notes B♭ and F♮ as you work the third fret. It opens in first position and then travels up the neck with a pentatonic scale until you reach the octave. Here, you play blue notes in a warbling riff at the fifteenth fret (the octave of the third fret). The progression shifts to D7 in measure 6 and then flows to the barred C at the fifth fret in measure 7. There you rise up to the B♭ (♭7th of C), so give it a little more energy.

The turnaround in measure 8 is a "piano-style" turnaround we played in an earlier arrangement, only now set in this tuning. Before you jump in, note in the tab how the numbers on the fourth string are descending and the numbers on the second string are ascending. The triplet on beat 2 is played with your ring finger on the F♮. On beat 3, you play a C chord like you would in standard. For beat 4, you play the E♭ with your index finger and the C♯ with your ring finger.

This is a G tuning workout for chording in the first position. It also presents a different 12-bar progression—one best described as IV–I–IV–I–V–IV–I.

As you practiced in previous lessons, the C7 is played as you would in standard, only the fifth string is open. The swinging groove is driven by the E♭ leading on the previous backbeat. Pick the open G and E♭ together with the thumb, and follow by strumming the chord. Then, pick the C on the second string and strum the chord again.

The following riff shifts in rhythm to a monotonic bass. The slide slashes at the fifth fret and then rests at the third. Note in measure 4 how the final F♮ in the phrase starts on beat 6 and sustains with vibrato over beat 7. Emphasis of the backbeat is a key feature of the blues, and phrases often start or end on an backbeat. The D7 chord opens up to include the open D strings; the chords are strummed with upstrokes of the index finger, as you played in the lessons with the monotonic bass.

This is blues from the Delta—a driving, monotonic bass on the bottom, with plaintive, expressive slide lines above. This is what it's all about. Remember, in open G tuning, the blue notes are all found at the third fret. This example opens up with a warbling line, alternating between D and F♯. Suddenly you stop in measure 2 and play just the bass. The warble kicks in again in measure 3, and resolves with the F on the first string in measure 4 to create a definite seventh-chord transition. Vibrato adds to the tension of the music.

The melody over the IV chord is created by using the slide to play octaves on the third and fifth strings. Use the slide to barre strings 5 to 1. Pick the strings indicated with your thumb and index finger. Measure 7 brings back the warble, this time resolving on G. The V chord melody is located entirely at the seventh fret, again created by a full barre with selective picking. In the style of the Black Ace, you move to the ♭VI (E♭7) instead of playing the conventional IV (C7).

Building on the theme of the previous lesson, this example opens at the fifteenth fret (the octave of the third fret), and with the slide, you walk triplets down to the twelfth fret (octave of the root). After four beats of the bass, you repeat this pattern. The technique over the IV chord is from the music of Son House, and is played without a slide; your index finger barres all of the strings. You come out of it with the slide on the B♭, and then repeat only to resolve back on the root in measure 7.

The phrasing over the D7 and C7 comes from the music of Muddy Waters. The triplet of G–B♭–D sets up the slashing chord notes four times before working back down to the first position G. Again, you reprise the warble riff from the previous lesson.

Open G tuning:
(low to high) D–G–D–G–B–D

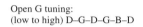

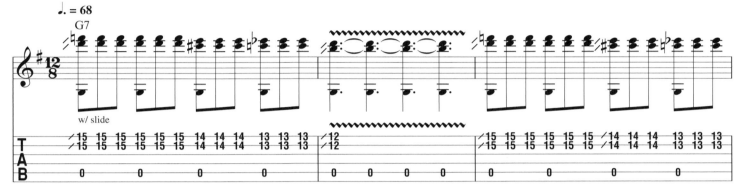

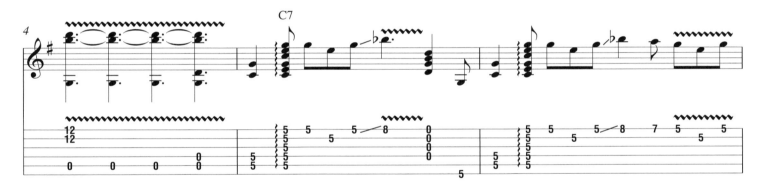

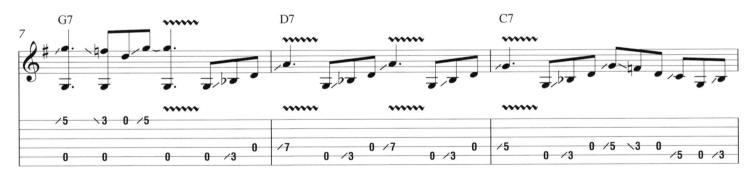

This lesson is an exploration of a loosely structured 8-bar melody, with a new groove that works well in open G tuning. It's inspired by the music of Son House, who played some of the finest blues from the Delta. "House" has been a profound inspiration to innumerable blues guitarists. His music is raw and sensual, perfectly encapsulating the power and magic of the solo performer.

First, let's look at the groove: a rhythm riff (as demonstrated in measures 1–2) counted as 1-& 2-e-& 3-& 4-e-&, with the thumb picking the bass on the downbeats. Beats 2 and 4 are syncopated, picking first with the thumb, then the index finger on the open third string, and then downstroking with the thumb again on the third and fourth strings as you slash the slide at the third fret. This pattern may repeat as many times as you wish. The melody then begins with the music in measure 3.

The melody is basically single-string with the rhythm riff filling between the lines. Riffs like the one at the end of measure 3 are slides that "curl around." Pick and slide into the first note, and then slide back, picking the open string on the backbeat. The riff on beat 4 of measure 5 is played with a slide barre at the third fret, picking the second string with your index finger and the first string with your middle finger. By the eighth measure, you return to the rhythm riff for as many bars as you wish before returning to the melody.

As described in previous lessons, the Piedmont style of blues is a fingerstyle marked by an alternating bass. This time, you add the slide to the mix. In open G tuning, the bass root is on the fifth string. For the alternating bass, you pick the open fifth string (G) and the open fourth (D). This requires practice to train your muscle memory. The first two measures set the pace and give you practice.

The syncopation of the melody, combined with the bass, takes time to master. It helps to count the rhythm before you try to play it. For the timing of measure 2 count: 1-e-&-a 2-& 3-e-&-a 4-e-&-a. With the slide on the second string at the tenth fret, pinch the fifth and second strings, slide up to the twelfth fret, pick the open fourth string, and then pick the first string (now covered by the slide at the twelfth fret). Throughout, your thumb maintains a pulse, alternating fifth string to fourth. Be careful not to cover the fourth string with the slide, as the bass note needs to ring out. The slide notes are either on pinches or between the beats of your thumb; most are between. Practice slowly and carefully.

The melody over the IV (C) and V (D) comes from the barred chord positions at the fifth and seventh frets, respectively.

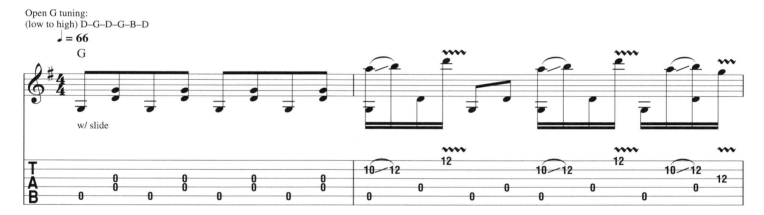

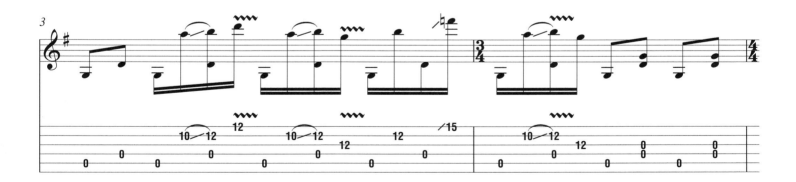

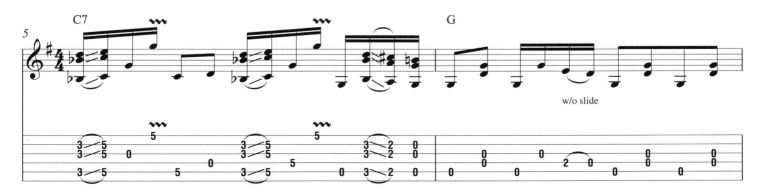

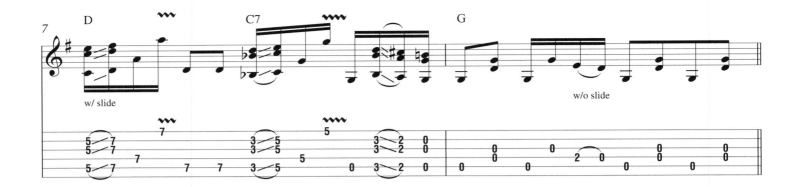

OPEN D TUNING

Open D Shuffle Beginner
Track 67

Among the different tunings used in the blues, "Spanish" and "Vastapol" are the most popular. "Vastapol" is also called open D tuning, and it really represents a family of related tunings. The name comes from a popular 1920s-era parlor instrumental, "The Siege of Sevastopol," which was played in this tuning: D–A–D–F♯–A–D (low to high). Tune the first and sixth strings down to D, the third string down to F♯, and the second string down to A. Some performers prefer open E, which requires tuning the fifth string up to B, the fourth string up to E, and the third string up to G♯. You can play exactly the same licks in either tuning, but open D has less tension on the strings and neck, and sounds a whole step lower.

This lesson will get you started. It's not a slide piece, but a fingerstyle shuffle arrangement in the key of D to acquaint you with the tuning. I've added a twist, breaking the last beat of each bar into triplets, with the high D splitting the bass.

As in open G tuning, the IV chord is a barre at the fifth fret and the V chord is a barre at the seventh fret. Play the G with an index-finger barre across all of the strings at the fifth fret. Beat 4 is once again split in rhythm with a quick C chord between the bass notes.

You'll recognize the turnaround on this one. This tuning presents it on the bass strings instead of the treble, but the intent and effect are the same. I play the line with my middle finger on the fifth string and my ring finger on the third, pinching them with my thumb and index finger, and picking the open D (first string) with my middle finger.

Open D tuning:
(low to high) D–A–D–F♯–A–D

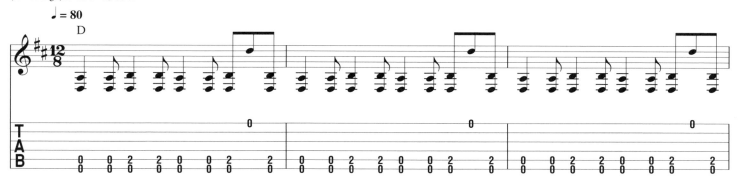

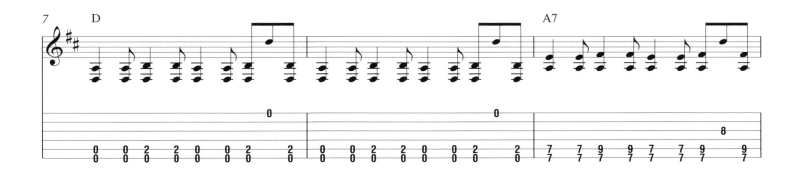

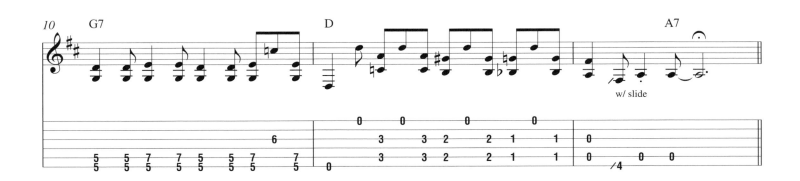

This is an exploration of open D tuning and what it has to offer. Just like in open G, the third fret is the post where you'll find the blue notes in the D blues scale: F♮ (♭3rd) and C♮ (♭7th). The opening line may be played with your thumb. In measure 3, you play a rhythm riff that fills between the melodic lines. On beats 2 and 4, pick the open A, slash the slide to play the C, and pick the open D on the fourth string.

Measures 5 and 6 reprise the melody, only an octave higher in the first position. If you read the TAB, you'll find this melody line reads very close to the line in measures 1 and 2. The parallels of the tuning (the strings tuned to A and D) allow you to play in two different octaves using the same fingering and fret position.

The pull-off on beat 4 of measure 6 is executed by picking the G and then lifting your finger to sound the F♯. The opposite effect is executed with a hammer-on at beat 4 of measure 9. Pick the open A and then forcefully fret the B (without picking it). Notice the directions in the music for the mixing of slide usage and standard fretting.

This piece, inspired by the great Tampa Red, is a mix of bass, melody, and chords. His single-string slide lines were always clean and expressive, earning him the title of the "Guitar Wizard."

The chords and double stops are frailed with the nails on your middle and ring fingers. The exception is the A7 chord in the turnaround, which is picked with upstrokes of your index finger. The chord substitution of the Gm for the G7 in this 8-bar blues (measure 4) is a feature of many 1920s-era arrangements.

In measure 1, perform a long slide down from the ninth fret (you may lift the slide around fret five) to the open string, and then slide back up to the fourth fret. A similar line appears in measure 3, only it resolves on the D at the fifth fret. The phrasing in measure 7 sounds complex but it is easy to execute. Fretting the notes with your fingers, pull off the E to the open D on beat 2. Use the slide to swing the triplet on beat 3 and pull off the G to the open F# on beat 4.

Another groove from the Delta, this is similar to a previous lesson, only this time in the open D tuning. Like many of the other arrangements, this one features a repeating rhythm riff that holds it together. In measure 1, the bass strikes on the first and third beats. Between the beats, the open strings and the slide on the C♮ chime in, and the pull-off on the third string drops the melody back down to the bass.

This melody was inspired by the singing of Skip James, from Bentonia, Mississippi. I'm fascinated by his range—the way he could start a song low and dark and then rise up into his "false voice," or falsetto. The slide on the guitar string, unrestrained by the frets, is capable of singing, creating melodies that flow and soar. It can also reach notes that frets cannot—notes "between" the frets which are critical for the blues singer searching for dissonance. And like the human voice, you sustain a note with a controlled vibrato.

Like so many lessons before, the melody can be broken down into "verses." The most common form of blues poetry is the AAB, and this music follows that format. The melody here is like a verse. Then it's repeated and subsequently resolved with a line that surpasses the previous two.

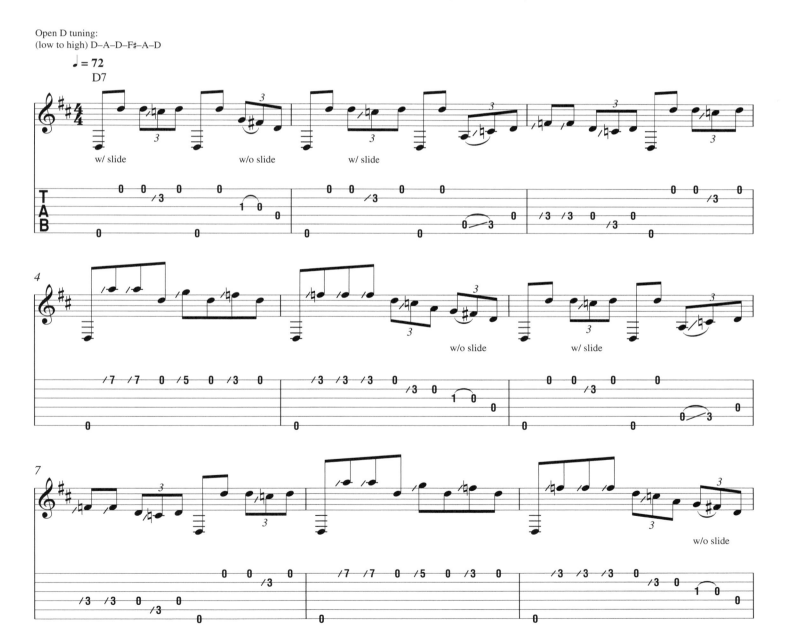

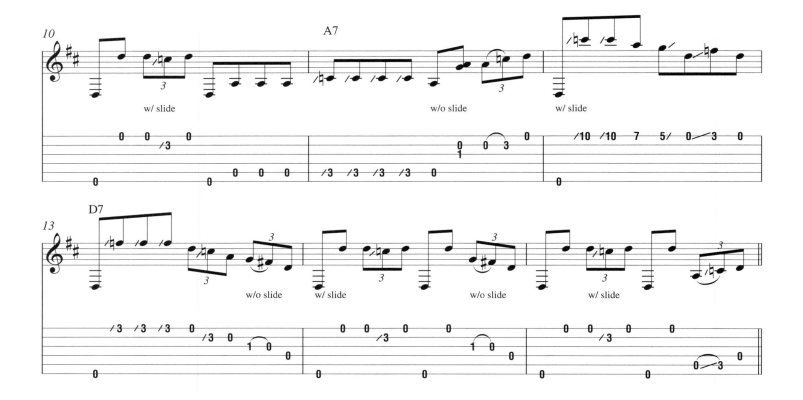

Born in the Delta #2

Track 71

Beginner

This is another one that my colleagues call a "gut bucket" blues because it's "roots" and raw. This one recalls the work we did earlier on the Lightnin' Hopkins inspired material, only now with the open D tuning, the music is darker and deeper.

Here we revisit some basic qualities of the tuning: the I chord (D) is played with open strings; the IV (G) is played with a six-string barre at the fifth fret; the V (A) is played with a six- string barre at the seventh fret; and the blue notes are found at the third fret.

This arrangement features a mix of slide and fretted notes. The opening phrase is fretted with your fingers. I want the open first string to ring out along with the open fourth; you can't do that with a slide. This makes the slide even more dramatic when it rises to the fifth fret in measure 2, and hovers with vibrato. This opening statement repeats throughout as the fill and holds the arrangement together.

In measure 8, the slide comes up on the F♮ and then resolves to D on the second string. You could play that D as the open first string, but it's more expressive as a slide note sustained by vibrato—it sings.

Open D tuning:
(low to high) D–A–D–F#–A–D

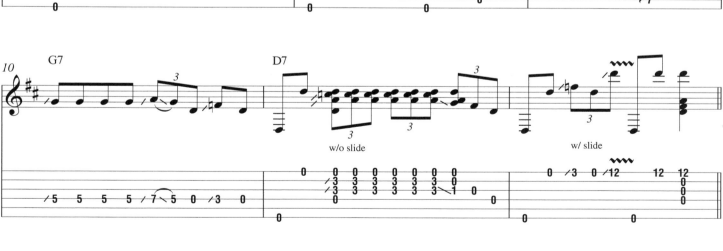

Once you acquaint yourself with this tuning, you'll discover the sounds created by the parallel D and A strings. This groove is created by working the parallels into an octave bass run—one I hear in a lot of Mississippi music. This is a fingerstyle arrangement where I use the slide to make small statements in between the verses. I pinch the sixth and fourth strings with thumb and index finger, and then pick the third string with my index finger.

By the end of the fifth measure, the bass walks up to the G at the fifth fret, but then drops back to the first position to play the bass line. Returning to the D7 in measure 8 is yet another form of the chromatic "walk-down" we've played on so many other arrangements. It sounds different because the notes are on adjacent strings, and the 5th is on top of the 3rd.

Open D tuning:
(low to high) D–A–D–F♯–A–D

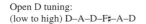

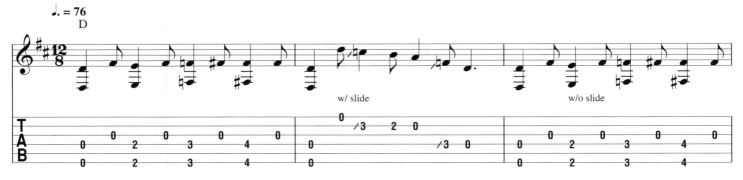

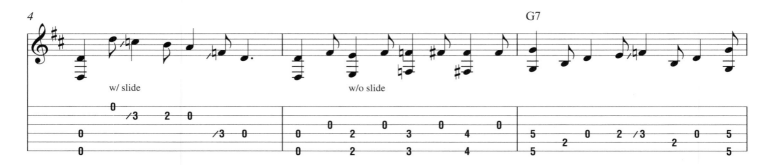

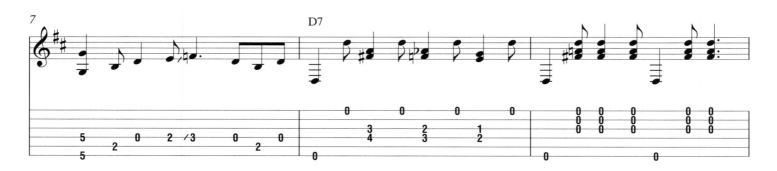

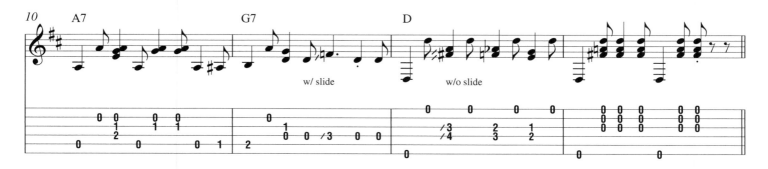

I couldn't resist another groove. This one walks the bass down with the open-D first string droning above (a good effect). Try playing the line with and without the drone and you'll hear the difference. That high note chiming in appears to fill out the "ghost" chord in between. This is primarily a fingerstyle arrangement with slide added to the fills.

Note the G chord in first position without the slide. You fret two notes: G on the third string and B on the fifth string. Rocking the bass from the ♭3rd to natural (B♭ to B) is a blues thing. It makes the rhythm swing! You hear this technique on much of the pre-war blues, guitar, and piano.

Rocking the slide between the D and C♯ (beat 4 of measure 7) also creates a tension. The C♯ likewise jumps out on the slide line in measure 11. Many players want to flat the C♯ (the seventh) to create the blue note, C♮, but keeping it sharp makes it unique and adds interest to the music. Listen carefully to some of the old stuff and you'll hear players alternating between the flatted and dominant notes.

The V (A7) chord in this tuning (see measure 9) is a fretted E and G sandwiched by open A strings. Inverting the seventh chord and playing the ♭7th in the middle of the chord creates a different sound and texture.

Open D tuning:
(low to high) D–A–D–F♯–A–D

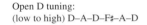

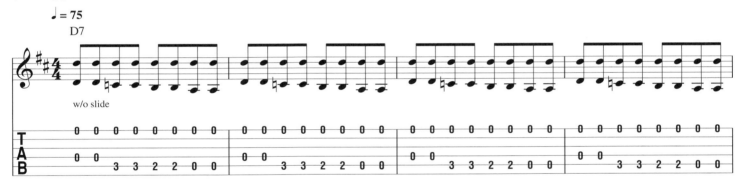

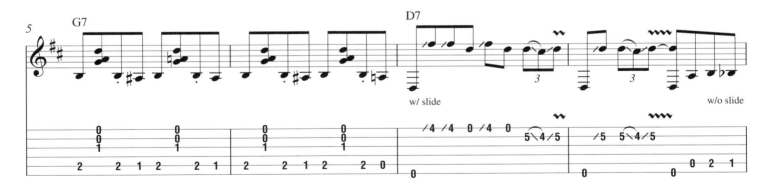

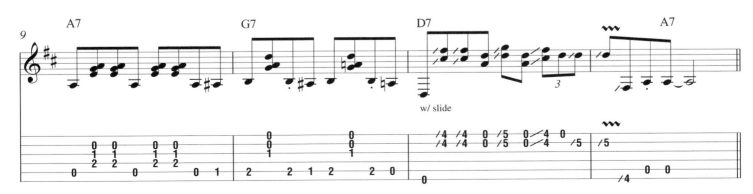

You can't play bottleneck slide without adding some Elmore James to your repertoire. The "King of Slide" covered Robert Johnson's "Dust My Broom" in 1951, and has been copied by countless players since. His signature was playing at the octave (the twelfth fret), a technique he applied to every one of his recordings.

This arrangement opens at the octave with a double stop. Then a flourish walks the line down to D on the fourth string. Aside from sliding down to the C (♭7th) on the first string, all of the notes are found at the twelfth fret—you need not wander far. The slides are short and quick. The technique on the last beat of measure 1 is critical, as you slide down and then back up on the lower string. This technique repeats not only in this arrangement, but so many others as well.

In transition to the G7, you jump high on the first string to the fifteenth fret for the F♯ (♭7th of G). This creates more than the usual tension of a blue note. Dropping back to the D, you play a half-step quiver, recalling the technique in the previous lesson of mixing the use of the C♯ and C♮.

The tension of the piece builds to the machine-gun climax in measure 10 with the rapid back and forth slide action between C and D. The phrase resolves with the curling riff mentioned above. The turnaround is all Chicago, with the chromatic walkdown, this time played with the popular octaves created by this tuning.

Open D tuning:
(low to high) D–A–D–F♯–A–D

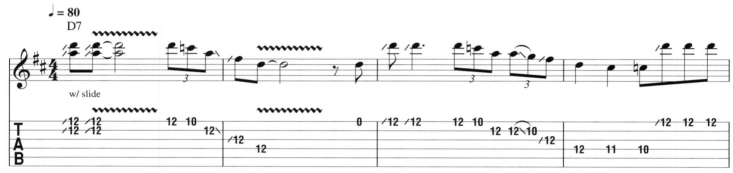

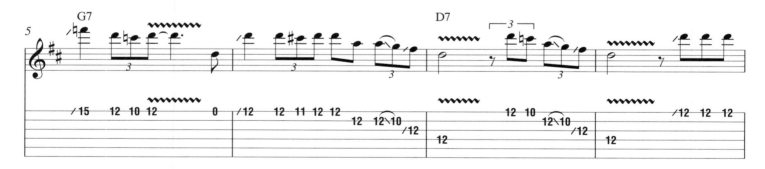

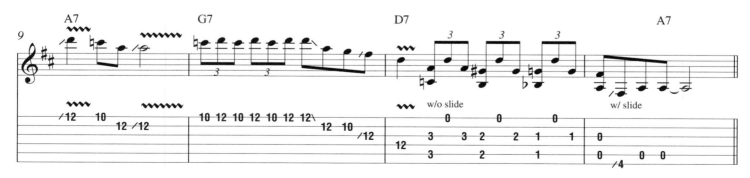

This arrangement expands on the previous one, working the slide riffs faster and harder. You will note the difference in the progression, as this is a 9-bar blues—a concept introduced earlier in the compilation. The pickups at the intro recall the alternation of the C♯ and C♮. The dissonance creates an interesting sound worth repeating in measure 1.

Some other techniques that are seen here contribute to the blues feel. At the end of measure 2, we'll jump ahead of the transistion, slashing high on the first string to play the bluesy F♮ (a beat-and-a-half before the chord change). The trill is another bluesy technique seen here in measure 7.

Track 76

The "Black Ace," (born Babe Turner), released the "Black Ace Blues" in the 1930s and later recorded it in the 1960s. He played lap-style slide like the Hawaiian players of the day. For this reason, some folks try to link Delta slide with Hawaiian music, but you can argue against it. Players were using knife and bottleneck slides at the turn of the twentieth century, long before recordings of Hawaiian music filtered into the deep south. Playing lap style presents its own set of skills, but it also creates new sounds—especially sweeping chords. You can achieve a similar effect by playing conventional guitar in the open D tuning.

The melody lines here are mostly on single strings. You start with a plaintive D sustained on the second string. In this "quick-to-the-four" progression, you slide a chord up to the G at the fifth fret. The melody rises and falls back to the root (D) and then you slash the slide—first up and then out of the twelfth fret, followed by the same curl at the fifth fret.

The return to the G7 in measure 5 is more sparse, laying down a monotonic bass before working up the fourth string. The phrase in measure 7 is a signature lick for Ace, highlighting the blue notes C and F. Another Ace feature is his chord transition in measure 10. Instead of holding at the G7, he would split the measure with the ♭VI (B♭7). This was a popular arrangement technique in the blues of the twenties, and Ace used it on almost all of his recordings!

Piedmont Slide
Track 77

Advanced

Before diving into this one, you should master the lessons in the fingerstyle section. Maintaining a steady, alternating bass is key before you can add the slide. The thumb alternates bass notes between the sixth and fourth strings throughout. The technique is more difficult in measure 3. The slide melody begins as you pinch the sixth and first strings. Count the beats as 1-& 2-& 3-e-&-a 4-&. On beat 3, you slide down from the F♯ before your thumb alternates on the bass. Measures 4 and 5 repeat the pattern, but resolve higher in the scale.

In measure 7 (beat 4), you pinch the open A and D, hammer on the B, and then pinch the open D (fourth string) and open D (first string). Beat 3 of measure 8 is syncopated, as you pinch the C♯ and the bass, slide down a half step, alternate the bass, and pick the open A. After repeating this phrase, you take it out by returning to the original pattern, pinching slide notes on the downbeats.

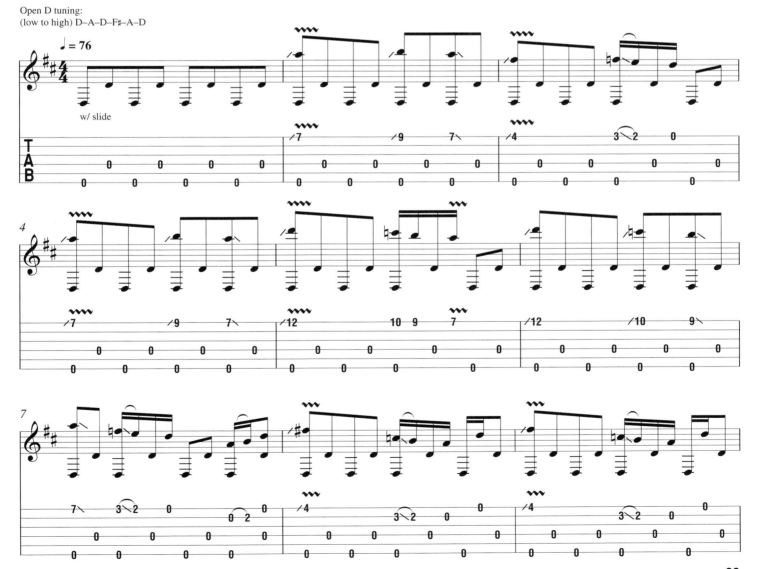

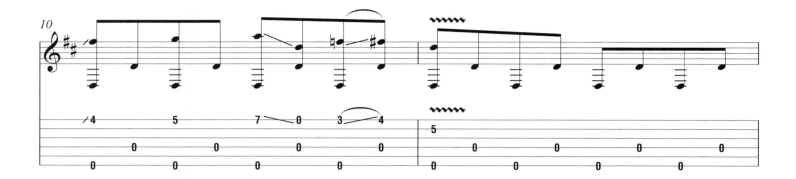

Mississippi Hill Country

Track 78

Advanced

One of my favorite performers in this tuning is Mississippi Fred McDowell. Like so many performers who settled in the northern hill country of Mississippi, his style created a rolling flow of music like the hills themselves. In the Piedmont style, the bass is alternating and churning while the slide attacks the strings. The basic rhythm here is 1-&-a 2-e-& 3-e-&-a 4-&.

The slide strikes the first string at the F♮ (third fret), nudges it up almost to F♯, and finishes on the second-string D (fifth fret). The rolling third beat starts with a pinch and pull-off before alternating the bass and adding the D on top. This rhythm riff has two parts. In the first part, beat 4 starts on the C♮. In the second, beat 4 is just the alternating bass. The two measures combined make the repeating phrase. You can play it and repeat it as much as you want. It sets the dance rhythm for you—the one-man band.

The progression simply alternates between the IV (the verse) and the I (the rhythm riff). There is no set limit of bars. You may extend or shorten passages as you play. Unlike everything else in this collection, this arrangement is loose and free flowing. Once you get the dancers moving, you don't want to stop!

The verses in this piece take place over the IV chord, with their own rolling rhythm. I find it necessary to break the previous rhythm before jumping into the new. A one-beat measure, with just the alternating bass, gives you the time to regroup. The rhythm rolls on the A chord in the first position, with a walking bass line on the final beat to define the measures.

After two measures, the progression resets with two beats and returns to the top for the second line in the verse. For the third line, I chose a different attack, slashing at the blue notes at the third fret and sliding out. For each phrase like this, set it up with the hammer-on from the fifth string open to the C♮.

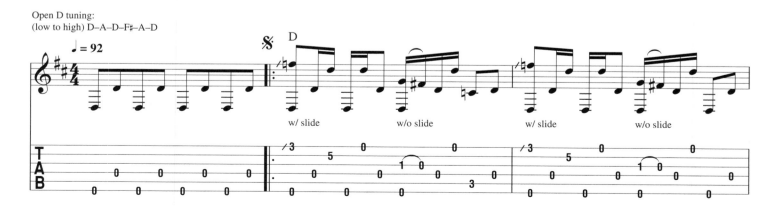

GUITAR NOTATION LEGEND

Guitar music can be notated three different ways: on a *musical staff*, in *tablature*, and in *rhythm slashes*.

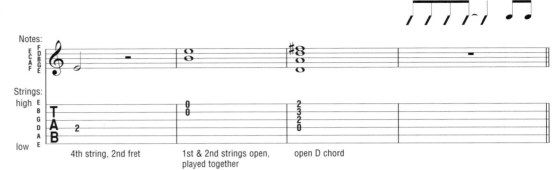

RHYTHM SLASHES are written above the staff. Strum chords in the rhythm indicated. Use the chord diagrams found at the top of the first page of the transcription for the appropriate chord voicings. Round noteheads indicate single notes.

THE MUSICAL STAFF shows pitches and rhythms and is divided by bar lines into measures. Pitches are named after the first seven letters of the alphabet.

TABLATURE graphically represents the guitar fingerboard. Each horizontal line represents a string, and each number represents a fret.

4th string, 2nd fret

1st & 2nd strings open, played together

open D chord

HALF-STEP BEND: Strike the note and bend up 1/2 step.

WHOLE-STEP BEND: Strike the note and bend up one step.

GRACE NOTE BEND: Strike the note and immediately bend up as indicated.

SLIGHT (MICROTONE) BEND: Strike the note and bend up 1/4 step.

BEND AND RELEASE: Strike the note and bend up as indicated, then release back to the original note. Only the first note is struck.

PRE-BEND: Bend the note as indicated, then strike it.

VIBRATO: The string is vibrated by rapidly bending and releasing the note with the fretting hand.

WIDE VIBRATO: The pitch is varied to a greater degree by vibrating with the fretting hand.

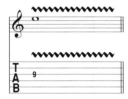

HAMMER-ON: Strike the first (lower) note with one finger, then sound the higher note (on the same string) with another finger by fretting it without picking.

PULL-OFF: Place both fingers on the notes to be sounded. Strike the first note and without picking, pull the finger off to sound the second (lower) note.

LEGATO SLIDE: Strike the first note and then slide the same fret-hand finger up or down to the second note. The second note is not struck.

SHIFT SLIDE: Same as legato slide, except the second note is struck.

TRILL: Very rapidly alternate between the notes indicated by continuously hammering on and pulling off.

TAPPING: Hammer ("tap") the fret indicated with the pick-hand index or middle finger and pull off to the note fretted by the fret hand.

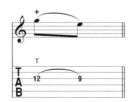

NATURAL HARMONIC: Strike the note while the fret-hand lightly touches the string directly over the fret indicated.

PINCH HARMONIC: The note is fretted normally and a harmonic is produced by adding the edge of the thumb or the tip of the index finger of the pick hand to the normal pick attack.

PICK SCRAPE: The edge of the pick is rubbed down (or up) the string, producing a scratchy sound.

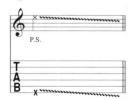

MUFFLED STRINGS: A percussive sound is produced by laying the fret hand across the string(s) without depressing, and striking them with the pick hand.

PALM MUTING: The note is partially muted by the pick hand lightly touching the string(s) just before the bridge.

RAKE: Drag the pick across the strings indicated with a single motion.

TREMOLO PICKING: The note is picked as rapidly and continuously as possible.

VIBRATO BAR DIVE AND RETURN: The pitch of the note or chord is dropped a specified number of steps (in rhythm), then returned to the original pitch.

VIBRATO BAR SCOOP: Depress the bar just before striking the note, then quickly release the bar.

VIBRATO BAR DIP: Strike the note and then immediately drop a specified number of steps, then release back to the original pitch.

MASTER THE *Blues*

With guitar instruction from Hal Leonard

All books include notes and tab.

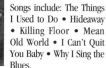

Hal Leonard Guitar Method – Blues Guitar
by Greg Koch

The complete guide to learning blues guitar uses real blues songs to teach you the basics of rhythm and lead blues guitar in the style of B.B. King, Buddy Guy, Eric Clapton, and many others. Lessons include: 12-bar blues; chords, scales and licks; vibrato and string bending; riffs, turnarounds, and boogie patterns; and more!
00697326 Book/CD Pack $16.99

Blues Deluxe
by Dave Rubin

Not only does this deluxe edition provide accurate transcriptions of ten blues classics plus performance notes and artist bios, it also includes a CD with the *original Alligator Records recordings* of every song! Tunes: Are You Losing Your Mind? (Buddy Guy) • Don't Take Advantage of Me (Johnny Winter) • Gravel Road (Magic Slim) • Somebody Loan Me a Dime (Fenton Robinson) • and more.
00699918 Book/CD Pack.....................$24.99

Art of the Shuffle
by Dave Rubin

This method book explores shuffle, boogie and swing rhythms for guitar. Includes tab and notation, and covers Delta, country, Chicago, Kansas City, Texas, New Orleans, West Coast, and bebop blues. Also includes audio for demonstration of each style and to jam along with.
00695005 Book/CD Pack.....................$19.95

Power Trio Blues
by Dave Rubin

This book/CD pack details how to play electric guitar in a trio with bass and drums. Boogie, shuffle, and slow blues rhythms, licks, double stops, chords, and bass patterns are presented for full and exciting blues. A CD with the music examples performed by a smokin' power trio is included for play-along instruction and jamming.
00695028 Book/CD Pack.....................$19.99

Lead Blues Licks
by Michael P. Wolfsohn

This book examines blues licks in the styles of such greats as B.B. King, Albert King, Stevie Ray Vaughan, Eric Clapton, Chuck Berry, and more. You'll progress from the standard blues progression and blues scale to the various techniques of bending, fast pull offs and hammerons, double stops, and more.
00699325..................................$6.95

Birth of the Groove
R&B, Soul and Funk Guitar: 1940-1965
by Dave Rubin

The years 1945-1965 saw a radical and exciting shift in American popular music. Blues and swing jazz helped to produce a new musical form called rhythm and blues, which in turn set in motion the development of soul and funk, not to mention rock 'n' roll. This book/CD pack explores everything from the swinging boogie of Tiny Grimes to the sweaty primal funk of Jimmy Nolen, and everyone in between. The CD includes 45 full-band tracks.
00695036 Book/CD Pack.....................$19.99

Electric Slide Guitar
by David Hamburger

This book/audio method explores the basic fundamentals of slide guitar: from selecting a slide and proper setup of the guitar, to open and standard tuning. Plenty of music examples are presented showing sample licks as well as backup/rhythm slide work. Each section also examines techniques and solos in the style of the best slide guitarists, including Duane Allman, Dave Hole, Ry Cooder, Bonnie Raitt, Muddy Waters, Johnny Winter and Elmore James.
00695022 Book/CD Pack....................$19.95

101 Must-Know Blues Licks
A Quick, Easy Reference for All Guitarists
by Wolf Marshall

Now you can add authentic blues feel and flavor to your playing! Here are 101 definitive licks – plus a demonstration CD – from every major blues guitar style, neatly organized into easy-to-use categories. They're all here, including Delta blues, jump blues, country blues, Memphis blues, Texas blues, West Coast blues, Chicago blues, and British blues.
00695318 Book/CD Pack.....................$17.95

Fretboard Roadmaps Blues Guitar
for Acoustic and Electric Guitar
by Fred Sokolow

These essential fretboard patterns are roadmaps that all great blues guitarists know and use. This book teaches how to: play lead and rhythm anywhere on the fretboard, in any key; play a variety of lead guitar styles; play chords and progressions anywhere on the fretboard, in any key; expand chord vocabulary; learn to think musically, the way the pros do.
00695350 Book/CD Pack.....................$14.95

The Road to Robert Johnson
The Genesis and Evolution of Blues in the Delta from the Late 1800s Through 1938
by Edward Komara

This book traces the development of the legendary Robert Johnson's music in light of the people and songs that directly and indirectly influenced him. It includes much information about life in the Delta from the late 1800s to Johnson's controversial death in 1938, and features fascinating historical photos, maps, musical examples, and much more.
00695388...$14.95

12-Bar Blues
by Dave Rubin

The term "12-bar blues" has become synonymous with blues music and is the basis for an incredible body of jazz, rock 'n' roll, and other forms of popular music. This book/CD pack is solely devoted to providing guitarists with all the technical tools necessary for playing 12-bar blues with authority. The CD includes 24 full-band tracks. Covers: boogie, shuffle, swing, riff, and jazzy blues progressions; Chicago, minor, slow, bebop, and other blues styles; soloing, intros, turnarounds, and more.
00695187 Book/CD Pack.....................$18.99

by John Ganapes
A comprehensive source for learning blues guitar, designed to develop both your lead and rhythm playing. Covers all styles of blues, including Texas, Delta, R&B, early rock and roll, gospel, blues/rock and more. Includes 21 complete solos; extensive instruction; audio with leads and full band backing; and more!
00695007 Book/CD Pack $19.95

by John Ganapes
A reference guide to blues, R&B, jazz, and rock rhythm guitar, with hundreds of voicings, chord theory construction, chord progressions and exercises and much more. The Blues You Can Use Book Of Guitar Chords is useful for the beginner to advanced player.
00695082 .... $14.95

by John Ganapes
A complete guide to learning blues guitar, covering scales, rhythms, chords, patterns, rakes, techniques, and more. CD includes 13 full-demo solos.
00695165 Book/CD Pack $19.95

by John Ganapes
Contains music and performance notes for 75 hot lead phrases, covering styles including up-tempo and slow blues, jazz-blues, shuffle blues, swing blues and more! CD features full-band examples.
00695386 Book/CD Pack $16.95

FOR MORE INFORMATION, SEE YOUR LOCAL MUSIC DEALER,
OR WRITE TO:

HAL•LEONARD®
CORPORATION
7777 W. BLUEMOUND RD. P.O. BOX 13819 MILWAUKEE, WI 53213

www.halleonard.com

Prices, availability, and contents subject to change without notice. Some products may not be available outside the U.S.A.

0710